children's
literature
in the
curriculum

LITERATURE FOR CHILDREN

Pose Lamb
Consulting Editor
Purdue University

Storytelling and Creative Drama—*Dewey W. Chambers, University of the Pacific, Stockton, California*

Illustrations in Children's Books—*Patricia Cianciolo, Michigan State University*

Enrichment Ideas—*Ruth Kearney Carlson, California State College at Hayward*

History and Trends—*Margaret C. Gillespie, Marquette University*

Poetry in the Elementary School—*Virginia Witucke, Purdue University*

Its Discipline and Content—*Bernice Cullinan, New York University*

Children's Literature in the Curriculum—*Mary Montebello, American University, Washington, D.C.*

children's literature in the curriculum

MARY MONTEBELLO
American University

Pose Lamb
Consulting Editor
Purdue University

WM. C. BROWN COMPANY PUBLISHERS
Dubuque, Iowa

Dedicated to
M. L. C.

contents

PART THREE: THE AESTHETICS

PART FOUR: APPENDICES

foreword

In this book, the focus is on the utilitarian function of the literature program for children, literature as it enriches and enlivens the curricula in language, science, mathematics, art, music, and the social studies. The author states the position that this is *not* the *only* role literature should play. Thus, included in this book is a brief section in which the curriculum in literature is discussed, much as it is discussed more thoroughly in another book in the series.[1] No reader is likely to ignore the author's eloquent plea for time in each school day devoted to literature; books selected because they are favorites, because they are excellent devices for teaching some facet of literary analysis or merely because the choice seems appropriate for the day, the time, or the place.

However, the major purpose of this book is to discuss and to illustrate the invaluable contribution trade books, and other media, can make to those areas of the curriculum in which the concern is not primarily for growth in literary understanding and appreciation. (The reader can supply *his own* definitions of these terms.)

The author clearly and effectively demonstrates how pupils' understanding and achievement in the language arts, mathematics, and almost every other curricular area can be enhanced through the skillful use of trade books. Authors and titles are listed, both in the text and in the appendices. Thus, this book should be a very useful and widely utilized reference source.

The book is organized in such a way that readers desiring specific information (e.g., what trade books are appropriate to use in conjunction with the mathematics program?) will find it easily available. Obviously, the titles and the authors listed represent only a portion of those books

1. Bernice Cullinan. *Literature for Children: Its Discipline and Content.* Dubuque, Iowa: William C. Brown Company Publishers, 1971.

which could serve to enlarge and enrich the elementary curriculum. The classroom teacher or team of teachers will need to work closely with the Media specialist in finding many other materials in addition to those discussed here.

Dr. Montebello has written with particular insight and enthusiasm about individualized reading. Such an approach to reading instruction cannot function without an adequate supply of learning media—print and non-print. The components of an individualized reading program are described and discussed, and teachers, both inexperienced and experienced, will have a much clearer concept of this freer, more child centered approach to organizing for reading instruction. She has included a discussion of *how* individualized reading programs operate as well as *why* she believes such a reading program to be effective. After reading this section of Literature for Children: Literature in the Curriculum, teachers will almost certainly have a more accurate concept of the rationale, the strengths and the objectives of individualized reading.

This book should convince even the most skeptical, textbook oriented teacher that the textbook, by itself, is not enough. Trade books, a significant element in a well-balanced, broadly conceived literature program, can and should enhance childrens' interest and achievement in every facet of the curriculum.

Pose Lamb, Editor

preface

The responsibility of this author was the treatment of children's literature in the elementary curriculum—using literature to accomplish objectives in other curriculum areas. However, it is neither this author's philosophy nor the intent to set the utilitarian value of tradebooks over and against their aesthetic value. Both utilitarian and aesthetic values are important. In the curriculum, literature should appear *as* literature as well as an enhancement and enrichment for other studies. It follows with this philosophy, that pupils would not be limited to one aspect or approach in literature presentation. The full development of man demands education not only of his intellect but also of his emotions, his imagination and his spirit.

Throughout the following chapters there are recommendations for the age-range of tradebooks. Please ignore those recommendations. Make your own decision. It is no secret that different reviewers assign different age recommendations to tradebooks. For example, one tradebook in this manuscript was assigned an "adults only" recommendation by one reviewer. Another said "ages eleven and up" while a third stated "all ages." All were notable reviewers talking about the same book. Thus, after reading a book, a teacher must make her own decisions in light of her unique knowledge about the youngsters with whom she learns.

When writing within a word limit, one can gloss over and write very briefly or try to write rather fully on the materials covered. In some sections the former has been chosen; in other sections, the latter. In either case, this author could not "tell all." But it is her wish to make someone want to *know* all. And if the reader wants to know more, then this book has achieved its purpose.

MARY S. MONTEBELLO

part

one

the
language
arts

chapter 1

the language arts

The language arts are here defined as the *receptive* language activities of reading and listening and the *expressive* language activities of speaking and writing. All the language arts are interrelated.

Language itself, how it is structured and how it works, is included in the language arts instruction. Grammar, vocabulary, dialect and usage matters, locating information, using a dictionary, proofreading, all receive attention. Listening, speaking, writing, are done for many purposes. And reading is regarded as more than simply a method for gaining meaning from the written word; literary study has a rightful place in the curriculum. Tradebooks are experienced for the literary merit of the story at hand as well as for supporting and enriching total curriculum studies. And the contribution of literature to the life of the child is equally important.

The language arts are the foundation of the school's program, for effective communication is essential to life and to living. We must be competent speakers and writers; we must be critical listeners and readers.

Linguistics and the Language Arts

There has been a movement in recent years for the inclusion of linguistics in language arts programs. Linguistics has been defined as "the scientific study of language."[1]

Lamb extends her "scientific study of language" with the statement, "Such study may concentrate on the sounds of language (phonology), the origin and changing meaning of words (etymology and semantics),

1. Pose Lamb, *Lingusitics in Proper Perspective* (Columbus, Ohio: Charles E. Merrill Publishing Co., 1967), p. 4.

or the arrangements of words in meaningful context in different languages (syntax-structural or transformational grammar)."[2]

The Nebraska curriculum guide defines linguistics as "the study of human speech; the units, nature, structure, and modifications of language, languages or a language including especially such factors as phonetics, phonology, morphology, accent, syntax, semantics, general or philosophical grammar, and the relation between writing and speech."[3]

Postman and Weingartner state that "any definition of linguistics depends upon who is doing the defining."[4] That is, to many teachers, the term linguistics is equated with grammar; to others, it is the relationship of sound symbols to graphic symbols. To many linguists, a definition broadened to include study of the entire culture is most suitable. To the man on the street, linguistics may mean the study of dialects or the determining of dictionary definitions. Postman and Weingartner go on to say, "Linguistics is a way of behaving . . . it is a way of behaving while one attempts to discover information and to acquire knowledge about language."[5] They discuss the behavior in terms of attitudes and procedures. Their emphasis is upon the inductive approach to learning, a spirit of discovery, a rejection of dogmatism, and the verifying and revising process identified with scientific study.

Linguistic study is done by linguists, though accepting the Postman definition means that anyone, including children in the elementary school, may do linguistic study if it is done in the spirit described.

Linguists, with their basic assumption of oral language, have stressed that language programs need to give greater attention to oral language than they traditionally have given. The legion of noteworthy tradebooks, the wide range of themes and plots, the numerous books which appeal to the varied and special interests of youngsters, the tradebooks without words, which are vividly and easily "read" through their illustrations—all of these, and more—provide a composite for oral language experiences. These experiences excite, for they are neither contrived nor deadly.

At the same time, however, the linguistic concerns of written expression must not be ignored. While it is true that writing is a derivative of speech, educators should not make a fetish of saying that lan-

---

2. *Ibid.*
3. The Nebraska Curriculum Development Center, *A Curriculum for English: Language Explorations for the Elementary Grades* (Lincoln: University of Nebraska Press, 1966), p. 2.
4. Neil Postman and Charles Weingartner, *Linguistics, a Revolution in Teaching* (New York: Dell Publishing Co., 1966), p. 3.
5. *Ibid.*, p. 4.

guage is speech. This is not to deny that speech is the language, but for school purposes, as opposed to the purposes the linguist has in his studies, it is convenient to refer to oral language and to written language. Tradebooks inspire vivid oral and written experiences.

Linguistics and Literature

In appendix six, there is an extensive bibliography of tradebooks about language and language study. As a result of linguistic study through tradebooks, youngsters can discover that

—words and expressions are coined to take care of the language users' needs;

—language changes and that it is continually changing;

—English has been changed by influxes of people and ideas;

—words have been brought into English from other languages;

—language has a historical development;

—language is a creative activity of each person;

—language varies with socioeconomic groups and geographical regions;

—there are numerous dialects;

—there are alternatives in pronunciation, word choice, phrasing, and construction;

—there is a sound (phonology) of language, a music of language;

—there is an evolution of the spelling of language as well as changes in spellings;

—words have origins, and they can discover the sources of those origins;

—there are varieties of definitions and that this is the most important branch of linguistics—semantics.

Through the wise use of tradebooks, youngsters may come to appreciate, understand, and use their language better. There will be an appetite and a zest for language and language learnings. There will be a greater feeling for effective communication.

chapter 2

language and vocabulary development

Often, there is a wearisome weltering of repetition in the child's selection and use of words. His language is flat and lusterless. But, in tradebooks are unfolded words and their meanings, origins of words, stories behind words, language concepts—and more. Introducing a child to these many facets of language will add luster not only to his language, but to his life as well. A sense of curiosity and wonder will be aroused.

Language development is enriched not only by books about language and words but by all of good literature. Appreciation for the well-chosen word or phrase or for a rich, descriptive passage is best accomplished by reading and discussing excellent literature. Children become aware of figurative language, symbolism, similes, metaphors, sentence patterns, and regional variations of language patterns as they experience good writing. After a story has been finished, the teacher and children may read particularly enjoyable words, phrases, or paragraphs. All of this makes a rich contribution to the child's language development.

Only as children are led to enjoy rich descriptive prose, the well-chosen phrase, and the stories behind language, will they become aware of the power of words. The total experience must be enjoyed though, for without enjoyment, no amount of books will make a difference in the language and vocabulary of their lives.

This chapter will introduce tradebooks that are rich with words, language, and concept power. There are two divisions to the chapter.

The first is entitled A Gaggle of Geese. The reader is shown what can be discovered from one book about words by taking that book a step backward in time. Then there are steps for moving forward as the many follow-up activities in which youngsters can become engrossed are explored.

In the second section, a raft of books about words and language is referred to, and suggestions are made for their continual use in the classroom. That section is entitled Wonders, Incorporated.

We begin with one book about words. Within the covers of that book, there are exciting learnings. But these are only the beginning. There are learnings about these words as one looks beyond the covers as well. As a teacher looks beyond the covers of a book, he is making linguistic discoveries which can then be shared with youngsters. In essence, he is saying to the youngsters that he is interested, too. He is saying that he has discovered some further information about the book they are reading or have read.

The reader will note linguistics permeating the following sections, as there is discussion or origins of words, semantics, dialects, a culture, and more.

A Gaggle of Geese

A GAGGLE OF GEESE.[1] In this delightful book composed of the phrases we have come to know as collective nouns, Eve Merriam has brought together twenty-six authentic terms. In the preface of her book, the author notes that all the terms are to be found in the *Oxford English Dictionary.*

A single book can be a point of departure to discovering treasure troves of magic. The author has just been on a long and exciting search that began with the aforementioned two books. The search went beyond those two books as one footnote led to another footnote. She learned that "gaggle of geese," "exaltation of larks," and many more than the twenty-six collective nouns listed in Miss Merriam's book are sparkling realities. They have come down to us from medieval books wherein proper young gentlemen were taught the precise designation for groups of their quarry. These collective nouns are little known, but authentic and poetic terms that have somehow disappeared.

One hopes that the fruits of the search will become part of one's being. If they do, it isn't just that we will be able to turn to someone and cooly and correctly say, "Look—a charm of finches." What is more important is that a magic of poetry will have quietly slipped into our lives.

The author wishes to share these fruits with her readers and hopes that they, in turn, will share them with youngsters.

1. Eve Merriam, *A Gaggle of Geese.* Illustrated by Paul Galdone (New York: Alfred A. Knopf, 1960). All ages.

It all began with the end of Sherlock Holmes. In 1906, having rid himself once and for all of Holmes and Watson, Sir Arthur Conan Doyle returned to the literary form with which he had begun his career fifteen years earlier, producing a historical novel, *Sir Nigel.*[2] In it, the young Nigel comes under the tutelage of Sir John Buttesthorn, the Knight of Dupplin, head huntsman to the King, and England's greatest authority on the hunt. In Chapter 11, the old knight says to Nigel, "I take shame that you are not more skilled in the mystery of the woods, seeing that I have had the teaching of you, and that no one in broad England is my master at the craft."

There follows a lengthy disquisition on the chase, with many anecdotes, illustrations, warnings, and exceptions drawn from his own great experiences, and finally, the knight says,

> "But above all I pray you, Nigel, to have a care in the use of the terms of the craft, lest you should make some blunder at table, so that those who are wiser may have the laugh of you, and we who love you may be shamed."
>
> "Nay, Sir John," said Nigel. "I think that after your teaching, I can hold my place with the others."
>
> The old knight shook his white head doubtfully. "There is so much to be learned that there is no one who can be said to know it all," said he. "For example, Nigel, it is sooth that for every collection of beasts of the forest, and for every gathering of birds of the air, there is their own private name so that none may be confused with another."
>
> "I know it, fair sir."
>
> ". . . And if you walk in Woolmer Forest and see a swarm of foxes, how would you call it?"
>
> "A skulk of foxes."
>
> "And if they be lions?"
>
> "Nay, fair sir, I am not like to meet several lions in Woolmer Forest."
>
> "Ay, lad, but there are other forests besides Woolmer, and other lands besides England, and who can tell how far afield such a knight errant as Nigel of Tilford may go, when he sees worship to be won? We will say that you were in the deserts of Nubia, and that afterward at the court of the great Sultan you wished to say that you had seen several lions. How then would you say it?"
>
> ". . . Surely, fair sir, I would be content to say that I had seen a number of lions, if indeed I could say that after so wondrous an adventure."
>
> "Nay, Nigel, a huntsman would have said that he had seen a pride of lions, and so proved that he knew the language of the chase. Now, had it been boars instead of lions?"

2. Sir Arthur Conan Doyle, *Sir Nigel* (London: E. Stock Publishing Co., 1906). Reprinted by permission of the Estate of Sir Arthur Conan Doyle.

"One says a singular of boars."

"And if they be swine?"

"Surely, it is a herd of swine."

"Nay, nay, lad, it is indeed sad to see how little you know . . . No man of gentle birth would speak of a herd of swine; that is the peasant speech. If you drive them it is a herd. If you hunt them it is other. What call you them then, Edith?"

"Nay, I know not."

". . . But you can tell us, Mary?"

"Surely, sir, one talks of a sounder of swine."

The old knight laughed exultantly. "Here is a pupil who never brings me shame! . . . Hark ye! Only last week, the young Lord of Brocas was here talking of having seen a covey of pheasants in the wood. One such speech would have been the ruin of a young squire at the court. How would you have said it, Nigel?"

"Surely, fair sir, it would be a nye of pheasants."

"Good, Nigel—a nye of pheasants, even as it is a gaggle of geese. But a covey of pheasants! What sort of talk is that?

What sort indeed! This quotation from Sir Arthur Conan Doyle makes a central point: the terms one discovers in *Sir Nigel* are genuine and authentic. Obviously, at one time or another, every one of these terms had to be invented—and it is equally obvious that much imagination, wit, and semantic ingenuity has always gone into that invention. What we have in these terms is clearly the end result of a game that amateur semanticists have been playing for over five hundred years.[3]

Some of the words in *The Book of St. Albans* have come down to this day, and are accepted, taken-for-granted figures of speech. What is most remarkable about this rich repository of poetry is that all the terms in it can be said to be correct, proper, and usable. The lyrical, fanciful "exaltation of larks" has credentials as good as the mundane and universally accepted "school of fish," since both terms offer as provenance the same source, the list in *The Book of St. Albans*. The most startling thing about the list is that not all of the terms in it refer to animals. Seventy of the terms refer to people and life in the fifteenth century, and every one of the terms makes the same kind of affectionate or mordant comment that the strictly field terms do.

And so one can certainly argue with good logic that every one of the terms found in *A Gaggle of Geese*, *Sir Nigel*, and *The Book of St. Albans* has an equal claim on our respect and loyalty. The fact that many

---

3. Most of these terms were codified in the fifteenth century. *The Egerton Manuscript*, the earliest surviving list of them, dates from about 1450; *The Book of St. Albans*, the most complete and important of the early lists (and the source for most subsequent compilations), appeared in 1486. A facsimile of *The Book of St. Albans*, by Dame Juliano Berners (London: E. Stock Publishers) appeared in 1881.

of them have slipped out of our common speech can only be described as lamentable. There is little enough poetry in our speech without our continuing to ignore a vein as rich as this.

The following list contains only a few of the terms found in *The Book of St. Albans*. While that book contains all the terms found in *A Gaggle of Geese*, they are not all repeated here. When they are, it is to add new information related to the term as found in *The Book of St. Albans*.

> *A Swarm of Bees*
> *A Plague of Locusts*
> *A Colony of Ants*
> *A Peep of Chickens*
> *A Paddling of Ducks on Water*
> *A Charm of Finches*

A Kindle of Kittens. Kin, kindred, and the German *kinder* are related to this word from the ME kindlen. To kindle literally means to "give birth."

A Rafter of Turkeys. Probably not what one might think, if one sees birds sitting on a beam. The term is related to raft in the sense of "a large and often motley collection of people and things, as a raft of books," according to Webster. It is also related to raff, which means a collection of things, and appears in some interesting variations, as riffraff and raffish.

A Gam of Whales. A whaling voyage could last as long as three years, and so when two whalers encountered each other on some remote sea, it called for a gam, an exchange of crews via whale-boats and the "gamming chair." It was a happy time for a whale-man and, obviously, the whales' habit of sporting playfully on the surface of the sea gave rise to this fanciful term.

A Rag of Colts. There has been considerable conjecture about this term. It may be related to rage; it may derive from the Old Norse rogg (from whence "rug"), meaning something shaggy (like a colt's coat). Hare conjectures that it is the word that became our word "rack," one of the gaits of a five-gaited horse.

> *A Skein of Geese in Flight*
> *A Gaggle of Geese on Water*

Space limitations of this paperback dictate that one needs to stop here. However, the foregoing list did not exhaust the list in *St. Albans*. There is more to unearth, to trace, to hunt, to scout out. The author has taken *A Gaggle of Geese* one step beyond that tradebook. Ths reader and his youngsters can go even farther. Senses can be sharpened as magic is restored to the mundane.

And now that we have this information, what do we do with it? If we are to stimulate youngsters to be omnivorously word-hungry, we ourselves must know about the beginnings of words so that we may be storytellers about words and language. Every word has a "once-upon-a-time." When we go beyond a youngster's tradebook (A *Gaggle of Geese*) to seek further information and share that information with youngsters, we are encouraging them, by example, to do the same—to go beyond a book.

Perhaps it would be wise to take youngsters seriously. Begin with *St. Albans* or *Sir Nigel.* Consider one or several of the following possibilities: (a) share the information with the youngsters much as you would share or tell a story—it is a fascinating story—there could be dramatization in your voice as you play the roles of Nigel, Sir John, Mary, and Edith; (b) tape the story for them to hear over and over and over again; (c) type the story so that they may read it; or (d) do all three. In that way, they can listen-and-read. They will be smitten by the musical sounds of many of the terms.

As youngsters become familiar with some of the collective terms, have them go the logical step beyond and invent and create new terms to fit the world they know—"a giggle of girls," "a noise of boys," "a squeesh of galoshes," "a galaxy of astronauts," and on and on and on. In so doing, they offer new candidates for contemporary lexicon.

One may work with the collective terms in still another way. Lead youngsters to discover the various categories, or families, of terms. The order seems to break down into six families, according to the apparent original inspiration for the term. The six families are:

A. *Onomatopoeia:* for example, a murmuration of starlings, a gaggle of geese.
B. *Characteristics:* a leap of leopards, a skulk of foxes. This is by far the largest family.
C. *Appearance:* a knot of toads, a bouquet of pheasants.
D. *Habitat:* a shoal of bass, a nest of rabbits.
E. *Comment:* (pro or con, reflecting the observer's point of view) a richness of martens, a cowardice of curs.
F. *Error:* (resulting from an incorrect transcription by a scribe or printer, faithfully preserved in the corrupted form by subsequent compilers) a school of fish, originally "shoal."

As youngsters find or invent terms, the teacher should not indicate to which family the term should be assigned. The youngster should be allowed to decide whether a murder of crows belongs in the second or in the fifth family. These decisions are proper moves in the game of words and word-hunting.

Beginning with *A Gaggle of Geese, St. Albans,* and *Sir Nigel* seems to be a sure winner. Animals, knights, knighthood, intriguing spellings! Some youngsters will not be able to resist.

And as teachers in various parts of the United States encourage word interest, there will be further discoveries for youngsters as they share information. Children in certain localities have access to certain manuscripts and information that youngsters in other localities do not. (For example, the Egerton Manuscript is located in Pasadena, California.) And the communication—oral and written—will be underscored with meaningfulness and purpose.

Dictionaries are needed to help in the word-hunt. Numerous and diversified dictionaries. All sorts and all kinds. And they must be within an all-age range.

In addition to the *Oxford English Dictionary, A Dictionary of Chivalry,*[4] a 1969 publication by Grant Uden and illustrated by Pauline Baynes, would be an excellent accompaniment to the hunt related to *A Gaggle of Geese.* Detailed marginal drawings illuminate the more than 1,000 entries in this treasury of knighthood. For other word hunts, the *1970 Britannica Book of the Year*[5] should be added to the shelves. A few of the newer words in the English language listed in that book are "geep, lox, gox, vox, pop, bionics, firmware, mascons, mitniks, and the golden handshakes." And readers of all ages will be interested in a book that is in the process of being written, *A Dictionary of the Tuscarora Language.*[6] It is authored by Marjorie Printup, herself a Tuscarora.

But, of course, more than dictionaries are needed. The dictionary is only one step; that is, if we are interested in going beyond words—to ideas, concepts, language, a gestalt development. Total linguistic discoveries will only come as one "goes beyond," because as one hunts words, one dips into history, people, events, language, thoughts, culture, living—all importantly related.

It is a truism that not all youngsters are word lovers, even as all adults are not word lovers. But some youngsters will be—have the potential to be—with help from the teacher. In some classrooms, it may be more judicious to begin with small groups rather than with the total group. The other "tuner-inner-outers" will pick up some information, even as they are "not interested." At another time, one of them may come to the threshold, too.

---

4. Grant Uden, *A Dictionary of Chivalry.* Illustrated by Pauline Baynes (New York: T. Y. Crowell, 1969).

5. *1970 Britannica Book of the Year* (Chicago: Encyclopaedia Britannica, 1970).

6. For further information, write to Marjorie Phintup at Walmore Road, Sanborn, New York.

The teacher won't reach all youngsters in his class. If he reaches and touches just one, he has won! The author wagers it will be more than one.

Wonders, Incorporated[7]

The bibliography for this chapter lists a trove of books dealing with words and language—well over 100. Space limits discussion to only a very few of them at this time. The attempt here is to show the diverse offerings. But for a gestalt, the reader must note the bibliography. Otherwise he will have lost over 100 books about words and language. That would be sad for youngsters, because they must be drenched in words, literally soaked in them, to have the right ones form themselves into the proper patterns at the right moment.

Wonders, Incorporated is a treasure for the word lover. Christopher tours a big factory, Wonders, Inc., where are manufactured amazing assortments of items, such as time, space, mistakes, words, and figures of speech. In the first room, lines are assembled: borderlines, by-lines, hairlines, and sidelines. In another room, mistakes are made, from Tiny Errors to Colossal Blunders. In the Proverbs Section, a machine can make anything from an ounce of prevention to a stitch in time. And there is the verbotron machine with which Wonders, Inc. achieved the first splitting of the infinitive. To appreciate the book fully requires some recognition of a few common phrases and expressions that might not be familiar to a younger child. However, this witty fantasy could be the way to make them familiar.

ABC's of Space[8] is a good-looking and informative space primer. There are big, clear photographs and diagrams in a stunning red, white, and black layout. The writing is direct and the print large. Each letter gets two pages, with a term and illustration on each: A is for Apollo, a huge spaceship that took three men near the moon. It carried a smaller ship, the Lunar Module, in which two men landed on the moon. A is for astronaut, a man in a spaceship that goes far out from the Earth. He can walk in space. He can go to other worlds, explore them, and come back. Americans and Russians are both sending men into space. Younger children can enjoy this book and these pictures even if they cannot understand every word. And the highly informative text will help older boys and girls realize they ought not to overlook a book simply because it has ABC in the title. Isaac Asimov is a prolific writer—

7. Crawford Kilian, *Wonders, Incorporated*. Illustrated by John Larrecq (Berkeley, Calif.: Parnassus Press, 1969). Ages 6-9.
8. Issac Asimov, *ABC's of Space* (New York: Walker & Co., 1969).

a man of 7,560,000 words, according to an article in the New York Times on August 3, 1969—*Words from History, Words from Myths, Words from the Bible* and more (see bibliography).

A book that points out similarities in languages is *In the Park: An Excursion in Four Languages.*[9] Children who enjoy words will probably be intrigued by this even if they are not language students, since the park scenes feature such attractions as swings, bicycles, elephants, trees, pretzels, and flowers. The book has no story, just charming pictures (collage and gouache) showing assorted children and the words for each object repeated in English, Spanish, French, and Russian, so that it is possible to enjoy (and feel linguistically encouraged by) similarities—for example, "benches" and "bancos." *In the Park* can be used with younger children, but will probably be most enjoyed by those who are able to read it alone.

People Words,[10] by William Severn, is a collection of eponyms, words derived from names of people. Divided into such categories as Food and drink, Clothes and fashions, Science and invention, Mind and body, and Relations with others, the lively text includes both everyday words and some less frequently used terms chosen for their general interest. An index of names and of words is included.

Wonders in Words[11] explores the beginning of a host of terms. Words are grouped into chapters that describe terms having their beginnings in geography, in flowers, in proper names, in animals, in numbers, and in money. Included is a provocative chapter on slang in which the author discusses a little-noticed idea: that some slang expressions are almost literal renditions of standard words. For instance, "burned up" relates to "incensed," "double-talk" to "equivocating," "put-on" to "impose," "uppity" to "haughty." Nurnberg's thoughts are pointed up by the pen-and-ink drawings of Frederick W. Turton.

Would You Put Your Money in a Sandbank?[12] is a book that toys with homonyms, puns, and riddles. There is a section on silly questions ("Would you call a fisherman's catch his *net* results?"); there is another on nonsense conversations ("Toss me a piece of *stationery,* Joe. I want to write a letter"; "How can I toss it if it's *stationary?*"); there is still another on silly poems. The illustrations are by Abner Graboff.

9. Esther Hautzig, *In the Park: An Excursion in Four Languages.* Illustrated by Ezra Jack Keats (New York: Macmillan Co., 1968). Ages 7-9.
10. William Severn, *People of Words* (New York: Ives Washburn, 1966). Upper elementary.
11. Maxwell Nurnberg, *Wonder in Words* (Englewood Cliffs, N. J.: Prentice-Hall, 1969). Ages 12-16.
12. Harold Longman, *Would You Put Your Money in a Sandbank?* (Skokie, Ill.: Rand McNally & Co., 1969). Ages 6-9.

In *What's Behind the Word?*,[13] Harold Longman elaborates stories of the origins of thirty-nine words. He makes his stories interesting, although in at least one instance, he leaves a question as to authenticity. He tells us that "sincere" derives from the Latin *sine cera*, meaning without wax, and explains that Roman cabinetmakers who did not hide blemishes in the wood with wax turned out *sine cera* work. Dictionaries do not seem to go along with that explanation, and John Moore in *Your English Words*[14] maintains there is no evidence for it. Moore says that many times he has run across that wax business, though in the version he has heard, the writers of letters omitted to put wax on them, the suggestion being that if the letters were unsealed so that anyone might read them, they had to contain something of which the writer was not ashamed—hence straightforward, sincere. Nonsense, says Moore in effect. When authenticity is in question, interested boys and girls should be encouraged to seek out additional evidence to prove or disclaim—just as an interested adult would do. This is a part of the verifying and revising process of linguistics and the scientific method.

Isaac Asimov explains the etymology of 250 words in *Words from History*.[15] Each is a highly interesting and fascinating historical account. His list includes such relatively modern entries as "appeasement," "cold war," "fifth column," and "ghetto," the last of which, he correctly points out, has taken on a new meaning of slum areas to which racial minorities are confined, not *de jure* but *de facto*. The term "iron curtain," which is usually credited to Winston Churchill, was picked up, according to Mr. Asimov, by Churchill from Goebbels, the Nazi propaganda minister. Although this book may occasionally be employed as a reference work, its principal use will be as a source of delight with bounteous incidental benefits in the form of historical and linguistic tidbits. Books such as this one have the power to capture the imagination of many otherwise uninterested boys and girls.

The teacher will need to find ways to reinforce the many new words being met by youngsters. One highly resourceful way is simply to adapt any popular game for classroom use by using the words boys and girls are encountering as they pursue their unique interests. In vocabulary building, almost any popular game can be adapted for use in the classroom, for example, Fish, Checkers, Chess, Monopoly, and Bingo.

13. Harold Longman, *What's Behind the Word?* Illustrated by Susan Perl (New York: Coward-McCann, 1969).
14. John Moore, *Your English Words* (Philadelphia: J. B. Lippincott Co., 1962).
15. Isaac Asimov, *Words from History* (Boston: Houghton Mifflin Co., 1969). Ages 12-16.

Tradebooks themselves offer suggestions for word and language games.

Fun with Words[16] is a thoughtfully organized and thoroughly educational book. Maxwell Nurnberg demonstartes here that it is as easy to devise entertaining and amusing calisthenics for the mind as it is to pound vocabulary and spelling drills into it. There are abundant exercises that deal with grammar, vocabulary development, usage, spelling, punctuation, puns, etymology, and more. This book aids in the acquisition of skills that enable youngsters to handle the language effectively.

In *C D B!,*[17] a well-known cartoonist has used the old childhood game of making words out of the sounds of letters and numbers as the basis of a highly entertaining little book. With each puzzle, he provides a comically expressive cartoon as a pictorial clue; thus, C D B! takes on meaning when accompanied by a picture of a boy pointing out a bee to a friend, and S N-E-1 N? can be easily decoded when a drawing of a man standing before an open door with hat in hand appears below. Some of the puzzles are easy, some are difficult; the letters and numbers must be vocalized for understanding. Children will enjoy looking at the ludicrous drawings, breaking the "code," and composing similar puzzles of their own.

Word Games for Play and Power[18] by Shipley is a book about word play and the fascination of words. A second book[19] by the same author is written for adults but is also provocative for better students.

In *Perplexing Puzzles and Tantalizing Teasers,*[20] there are riddles, puzzles, mazes, and tricky word games. It is a clever and compulsive collection.

Drawing from his own knowledge, a teacher would be able to compose word-study paragraphs related to various subject-matter areas. In writing the paragraphs, there should be focus on a basic principle of learning and retention; that is, the seeing and showing of relationships. Thus the paragraphs would include not only the origins of words, the roots of words, but related words as well. To give an example, in social studies, an interesting pursuit would be to create paragraphs related to

16. Maxwell Nurnberg, *Fun with Words.* Illustrated by Ted Schroeder (Englewood Cliffs, N. J.: Prentice-Hall). Intermediate grades and up.

17. William Steig, *C D B!* (New York: Windmill Books and Simon & Schuster, 1968). Ages 8 and up.

18. Joseph T. Shipley, *Word Games for Play and Power* (Englewood Cliffs, N. J.: Prentice-Hall, 1962). Ages 8 and up.

19. Joseph T. Shipley, *Playing with Words* (Englewood Cliffs, N. J.: Prentice-Hall, 1960).

20. Martin Gardner, *Perplexing Puzzles and Tantalizing Teasers.* Illustrated by Laszie Kubinyi (New York: Simon & Schuster, 1969).

People in the Community, the many helpers, while investigating "iatrist." Or, in science, informative paragraphs would emerge as a result of tracking down the many "ologists."

The paragraphs could be typed and tape-recorded for listen-and-read experiencing by the youngsters. Once exposed to the paragraphs, several additional pursuits might occur.

Youngsters could be encouraged to rewrite any or all of the paragraphs. The rationale would be one or both of the following. First, in the light of additional or more current information that has been found, the paragraphs should be revised. Footnoting would be a reasonable and relevant expectation. Secondly, youngsters may discover "better" ways of "saying what we mean"—even better than the teacher's comments and notes. Great!

Youngsters could rewrite the paragraphs for boys and girls at grade levels below their own grade level. Children learn from one another. And, as the youngster is doing the rewriting, he would be refining his thoughts and concepts as he "verbalizes" his thoughts.

Boys and girls should compose their own paragraphs about word origins and related words resulting from their individual word-sleuthing and personal readings. The paragraphs could be typed or written by the youngsters. The same paragraphs could then be tape-recorded for listen-and-read experiences as well as for the listening pleasure of those who want to "hear" but who cannot "read."

There should also be listening and oral-expression experiences. The teacher should tape these paragraphs so that youngsters may listen to them as often as they so desire. The children should tape-record their pronunciations of the words. They could then compare their pronunciations with those of the teacher's. Continual oral refinement should be encouraged. Words take on a new dimension if one hears the words in his own voice; the words belong to him more intimately than if he merely hears and listens to the voice of another.

Youngsters are attracted by the birth and upbringing of words. This fact lends itself to encouraging interest in language and in enlargement of vocabulary. The intent, though, is not to separate or to set apart. A word belongs. It belongs in sentences, in paragraphs, and in total literary works. The total is important.

Language is like soil. However rich, it is subject to erosion, and its fertility is constantly threatened by uses that exhaust its vitality. It needs constant reinvigoration if it is not to become arid and sterile. The teacher needs to be the one important source for the maintenance and renewal of language. He becomes acquainted with a host of books about language and words and makes them easily accessible to youngsters.

He provides follow-up and reinforcing activities, creates activities himself, and encourages youngsters to be creative, too.

Throughout the total experience, there is a time for telling and a time for discovering. No author writing in some far-off place can tell the teacher "what" and "when." The teacher will make decisions appropriate to his own class.

chapter 3

oral expression

Books have the power to elicit oral expression by the absence of words and the presence of lucid illustrations.

Out! Out! Out![1] by Alexander is a book which encourages the child (ages 3-6) to tell the story from the pictures only. When a pigeon flies through an open window into the kitchen, a hullabaloo ensues as the mother, aided by a deliveryman and the janitor, pursues the pigeon from room to room, from cupboard to fireplace. Watching with obvious delight are two small children, one of whom succeeds in getting rid of the pigeon when the adults fail. All of this is told without words in expressive, action-filled pictures.

Another excellent example is *A Boy, a Dog, and a Frog*[2] by Mayer. With amusing pen-and-ink drawings, and without the aid of a single word, this book tells of the hilarious and unsuccessful attempts of a small boy and his dog to catch a frog—a frog that follows them home and into the bathtub. Youngsters from three to six years will be able to "tell" or "read" the story.

Bobo's Dream[3] is a charming tale of dreams of glory, in which the author uses no words. Her small black boy and his amiable dachshund, Bobo, make every action crystal clear. The boy, wearing his football helmet and jersey, is reading under a tree, having fed his small dog a large bone. Big dog appears, walks off with bone. Boy wrests it back. Adoring small dog gratefully licks boy. Then the dream: the boy is playing with his friends and some bigger boys catch and keep his ball; enormous in his fantasy, Bobo stalks majestically over and the big boys decamp in terror. Waking, the small dog sees the big one again, but this time he barks and the big dog cowers. The message

1. Martha Alexander, *Out! Out! Out!* (New York: Dial Press, 1968).
2. Mercer Mayer, *A Boy, A Dog, and a Frog* (New York: Dial Press, 1967).
3. Martha Alexander, *Bobo's Dream* (New York: Dial Press, 1970). Ages 3-6.

is either that bravery is all in the attitude, or that perfect love casteth out fear. In any case, the book should provide an effective stimulus to oral expression.

In *Frog, Where Are You?*,[4] boy has frog, boy loses frog, boy hunts frog and finds him installed as the smirking proud father of a large family, one member of which is taken as a substitute pet to the satisfaction of all concerned. There are no words in this beguiling little book, and none are needed; it is easy for children to follow the action and to appreciate the antics of the hero. The drawings are very funny, especially the one in which a companionable dog who has stuck his head irretrievably into the empty frog-jar peers hopefully about for the lost one.

In the picture book, *The Adventures of Paddy Pork*,[5] there is no text. Detailed black-and-white drawings tell the whole story. A young pig on his way to the store with his mother glimpses the circus going by and tries to follow it. He gets lost in a scary wood, barely escapes the clutches of a dissembling fox, catches up with the circus, proves most inept at performing tricks, and finally finds his way home to the welcoming arms of mother pig. The insertion of half-width pages between the full-width pages gives the delightful effect of opening doors, peering around corners, and uncovering surprises.

An absurd competition between two neighbors is presented in *The Winner*.[6] This is a whimsical, wordless picture book . . . sure to delight the very young.

Again, there are no words—just pictures for the youngest to "read" or "write" (dictate) about in *Making Friends*.[7] No words, but experiences and pictures that youngsters understand and can read.

"I won't take it!" says Little Brother when Mother brings his medicine. But he doesn't use words. He just covers his mouth. *Talking without Words*[8] suggests some of the many ways in which one can communicate without speaking or writing. In a series of black-and-white illustrations, the author shows the cautionary finger-to-lips that means "Don't wake the baby," or the elbow-hugging shiver that says, as plain-

4. Mercer Mayer, *Frog, Where Are You?* (New York: Dial Press, 1969). Ages 3-6.
5. John S. Goodall, *The Adventures of Paddy Pork* (New York: Harcourt, Brace & World, 1968). Ages 3-6.
6. Kjell Ringi, *The Winner.* Illustrated by the author (New York: Harper & Row, Publishers, 1969). Ages 3-6.
7. Eleanor Schick, *Making Friends* (New York: Macmillan Co., 1969). Ages 2-6.
8. Marie Hall Ets, *Talking Without Words* (New York: Viking Press, 1968). Ages 3-5.

ly as words, that one is cold. Children should find the idea fascinating and some of the examples very funny.

Then, too, there are themes that can make oral expression irresistible. Consider the following books.

World on a String: The Story of Kites[9] traces the history of kites from their unknown beginnings in China to the present. The author discusses the use of kites in science, sports, transportation, religion, and war, and she cites some strange and famous kite flights. An epilogue contains information on kite flying today, the five basic kinds of kites, where kites can be purchased, and kite clubs for children and adults. Suggestions for further reading are given, and the book is illustrated with old prints and photographs. Youngsters in third grade and up would have their own tales to relate after reading this book or having it read to them.

What Do I Say?[10] is a book suitable for children from ages four to six, and one that is sure to elicit responses from the child to whom it is read. Youngsters will readily identify with the child in this picture book—a little Puerto Rican boy living in a large American city. What Manuel does in the course of a day is realistically and appealingly pictured in colored and black-and-white illustrations. What Manuel says when he gets up in the morning, when he leaves for school, when asked his name, when he wants to swing, and in other situations all related in a minimum of words.

Say Something[11] by Mary Stolz will stimulate young readers from ages five to seven. Standing before an easel with blank paper and paints, a boy commands himself to say something about his world and obeys with imaginative observations in words and pictures. The cheerful wash drawings in red, blue, and yellow, along with descriptions of nature like "A tree is an apartment house where the catbird and cardinal can live for a song" is one of the many provocative descriptions.

But Where Is the Green Parrot?[12] is an amusing game rather than a story. In this picture book, a green parrot is to be found somewhere in each of nine full color double-page spreads; it is more carefully hidden in some than in others. The illustrations, showing among other things

9. Jane H. Yolen, *World on a String: The Story of Kites* (New York: World Publishing Co., 1969).
10. Norma Simon, *What Do I Say?* Pictures by Joe Lasker (Chicago: Albert Whitman & Co., 1967).
11. Mary (Slattery) Stolz, *Say Something*. Pictures by Edward Frascino (New York: Harper & Row, Publishers, 1968). Ages 5-7.
12. Thomas and Wanda Zacharias, *But Where Is the Green Parrot?* (New York: Delacorte Press, 1968). Ages 2-5.

a toy chest, a house, a train, and a garden, are large, clearly drawn, and pleasingly detailed, while the text merely describes the scene and asks the question: But where is the green parrot?

365 Things to Know[13] is an unusual book. Written and illustrated by Clifford Parker, it focuses on one question and answer a day. Quick now—"Why is Samuel Plimsoll remembered?" Don't know, eh? Try some others from this book: "When a letter is mailed, what happens to it?" "What is another name for a river horse?" "Why is a cat's tongue rough?" There is one question for every day in the year, along with ample, unhurried answers to each question. There are illustrations, too, lots of them, to expand the answers where necessary and to attract interest.

Things We Like to Do[14] would be especially helpful in Head Start and nursery school programs. Most of the scenes pictured in these photographs of black, white, and Oriental children at play will be familiar to preschoolers. The minimal text is simple. Together with the black-and-white photographs, set off by a bright red background, the book will surely bring on a natural flow of conversation.

A Handful of Surprises[15] recounts the adventures of Tink, Tark, Mac, March, and O'Tooley—finger puppets on the gloved hand of a clown. Illustrated with humorous line drawings, the antics of the five squabbling characters make a story that will lead young children to finger play and speaking.

Juba This and Juba That: Story Hour Stretches for Small Groups[16] is an entertaining collection of chants, rhymes, audience-participation and action stories, finger plays, riddles, songs, tongue twisters, and jokes which the author, a children's librarian-storyteller, has used with maximum success in the "stretch" periods of her story hours. Directions for leader and participants are given, and a note to storytellers is included. The book is illustrated with bright, humorous drawings. Children will enjoy "telling" and "playing" on their own.

Give the child much to hear and talk about—stories and ideas of all shapes, kinds, and sizes. Give him the happiness of hearing books. But let him express. Give him unhurried time to express, to tell from pic-

13. Clifford Parker, *365 Things to Know*. Illustrated by the author (Racine, Wisc.: Western Publishing Co., Golden Press, 1969). Ages 8-11.
14. Evelyn M. Andre, *Things We Like to Do* (Nashville: Abingdon Press, 1968). Ages 2-5.
15. Anne Heathers and Frances Esteban, *A Handful of Surprises* (New York: Harcourt, Brace & World, 1961). Ages 4-7.
16. Virginia A. Tashjian, comp., *Juba This and Juba That: Story Hour Stretches for Small Groups*. Illustrations by Victoria de Larrea (Boston: Little, Brown & Co., 1969). Ages 6-8.

tures, to express and comment during a story, and to talk about it afterward. He will—unendingly—but vitally!

The flannelboard should be used often. But let *the child* use the flannelboard. Let *him* use the puppets. Let *him* be the storyteller.

The educative process should be one of partnership. *Tell-Together Stories*[17] by Jean Lee Latham is a collaboration for the young. And the stories are just that. Each story begins, "Now here is a story for us to tell-together. I'll tell what happened, and you'll make the noises." And that is the way the stories go. And that is the way oral expression should begin. Together.

---

17. Jean Lee Latham, *Tell-Together Stories* (New York: Macmillan Co., 1966).

chapter 4

reading

Consistent use of children's literature in the reading program, both before they begin to read and at each step of the developmental process, should be characteristic of any reading program in the seventies. Tradebooks must be central in the instructional program in reading. During the readiness and initial reading period, tradebooks can help create a desire to read. An active desire to read is essential to the success of a child's first experiences in learning to read. Happy experiences with a variety of picture books will greatly enhance the development of a strong interest in books and a determined desire to read.

The many skills usually associated with readiness for reading can be developed and reinforced by using picture books. Reading aloud provides the variety of listening experiences. The child's auditory discrimination and interpretation can be increasingly refined. Because of the combination of written text and pictures in these books, the child's visual discrimination abilities are nurtured from seeing and interpreting the illustrations in picture books. Attending to visual details is thus pleasant and relevant. And concept and language development are nurtured.

The numerous comprehension and interpretation skills have the potential for being developed through the use of tradebooks. The literary quality of the writing, the racing climax of a plot, the problems of the characters, imagination—these and many more characteristics of fine tradebooks—make palatable and enjoyable the finding of the main idea, interpreting details, making inferences, and the like.

Individualized Reading

For children who are beginning to read, the number of noteworthy tradebooks now available makes individualized reading more practical than it had been previously. Children's interests can be satisfied and, at the same time, educationally sound teaching-learning experiences can occur.

> Individualized reading is primarily concerned with reading as it meshes into and promotes child development in its many different aspects—physical, mental, social, emotional, linguistic, and experiential. It is interested not only in a child's reading achievement but also in his interest in reading, his attitude toward reading, and his personal self-esteem and satisfaction in being able to read. The growing interest in dynamic psychology has called attention to the importance of motivation and levels of aspiration in learning activities.[1]

Willard Olson made several studies of growth, behavior, and development of children. He then synthesized the results of his studies and thinking into three terse terms: seeking, self-selection, and pacing. It is this crystallization of Olson's psychology which has provided the basis for most individualized teaching of reading in recent years.

Olson explained that a child is continually exploring his environment and seeking experiences that fit in with his growth and needs. These seeking inclinations, accompanied with self-selection of stimulating materials, are basic to learning. Pacing, in accordance with the child's own rate of growth, is equally important, according to Olson. Applied to reading, this would mean that the situation most conducive to reading growth would be one in which the child is surrounded with stimulating books which he can explore and from which he can select and read at his own rate.

Garrettson summarizes the individualized reading concept as follows:

> When a child is allowed to use material of his own choosing, move at his own pace, in an atmosphere where how he moves is no longer public classroom concern, he relaxes his defenses and begins to feel the security of accomplishment.[2]

Barbe's term is "personalized reading." He writes:

> Labels in themselves, have little meaning. Their goal should be to clarify rather than to confuse. Unfortunately, the term "individualized" has been given widespread recognition. But, as one author has pointed out, individualized reading is not a method. It may well be that this will distinguish the Personalized Reading Program,

1. Willard C. Olson, "Seeking, Self-Selection, and Pacing in the Use of Books by Children," *The Packet* (Lexington, Mass.: D. C. Heath & Co., Spring 1952), pp. 3-10.
2. Grace Garrettson, "How One School Reads the Needs of the Slow Reader," *Nineteenth Yearbook of Claremont College Reading Conference* (Claremont, Calif.: Claremont College Laboratory, 1954).

which is a distinct method, from the less specialized term "individu-alized."

As the title implies, personalized or individualized reading instruction is essentially a program which teaches the child how to read on an individual basis. As Jeanette Veatch states: "Briefly, this new reading program . . . is based upon the idea that children can and do read better, more widely, and with vastly increased interest, when allowed to choose their own reading materials. The self-selection principle discards the well-known idea of planned, sequential development of level of difficulty programs of basal readers."

In essence the program is one in which each child is allowed to select, from a wide range of materials, those books to read which he is able to read and which he wants to read. The teacher then instructs the child individually using this reading material of his own choice in necessary skills of word attack, comprehension, etc., without use of the traditional fairly static reading groups within the regular classroom.[3]

Veatch says:

In spite of some confusion as to its meaning, the term "individualized reading" has come to indicate a special way of teaching in the classroom. Unfortunately, while the term clearly emphasizes the quality of individual instruction unique to this practice, it also seems to imply that grouping never occurs. This, of course, is not the case, as there is extraordinary opportunity for wise and efficient grouping in such a program.

Another widely used term is that of "self-selection." Yet, it, too, is inadequate in its seeming denial of the instructional role of the teacher. Let no one think that this book deals with other than the major reading program in a classroom. The approach discussed in this book is not subordinate to or an adjunct of the common basal reading program—what we are considering here *is* the basic instructional program.

As such it has certain prime characteristics that occur regardless of the variations in practice found throughout the country. These are: (1) self-selection of material by pupils for their own instruction, (2) individual conferences between each pupil and teacher, and (3) groups organized for *other* than reasons of ability or proficiency in reading.

Many teachers confuse an individualized approach and recreational reading because both entail self-selection of books. The difference lies in the *instructional* role of the teacher. For example, in recreational reading, we find the following:

> A weekly or biweekly period
> Little or no actual instruction

---

3. Walter B. Barbe, *Educator's Guide to Personalized Reading Instruction* (Englewood Cliffs, N. J.: Prentice-Hall, 1961), pp. 14-16.

> Teacher largely free and inactive once books are chosen
> Little attention to skill development
> Reading entirely silent.

A quite different picture is found in the individualized approach:

> A daily reading period
> Continual instruction
> Teacher active and in demand
> Concern for skills development
> Reading silent with frequent opportunities to read orally
> to the teacher and to the class.[4]

And according to Jenkins:

> The thing which troubles me about individualized reading is teachers' assumption that it is one thing. Actually, it is many things, for it is individual guidance in reading. As such, it varies from teacher to teacher, from pupil to pupil.[5]

There are certain prerequisites for involvement in an individualized reading program, the major one being that the teacher believe in individualized reading. He must have a thorough knowledge of tradebooks, the reading process and the know-how of methods and activities for developing various phases of that process.[6] He should maintain an ongoing file of ideas that will contribute to the development of all phases of the reading process. There should be a willingness to add continually to his knowledge of children's books, and there should be a determination to make a squirrel's hoard of books available and easily accessible to youngsters. Research has shown that accessibility of literature is the most important influence on reading.[7]

Individualized reading does not mean a teacher abdicates his role in shaping instruction. He has a definite role, and there are preliminary steps to be taken before beginning the program.

Sources of Tradebooks

The teacher needs to secure a multitude of tradebooks. Several sources for tradebooks are available. The elementary school library, the neighborhood and central public libraries, state libraries, bookmobiles, children's book clubs, the recreational and unit libraries made

4. Jeanette Veatch, *Reading in the Elementary School* (New York: Ronald Press Co., 1966).
5. William A. Jenkins, "Reading Skills in Teaching Literature in the Elementary School," *Elementary English* 41 (November, 1964):778-82.
6. An excellent source for the Reading Process and the "know-how" involved therein is *On Their Own in Reading* by William S. Gray (Glenview, Ill.: Scott, Foresman & Co., 1960). Gray notes four phases to the process and gives detailed methods for fulfilling these phases.
7. Norine Odland, *Teaching Literature in the Elementary School* (Champaign, Ill.: National Council of Teachers of English, 1969), p. 25.

available to teachers (books often given to teachers for long-term loan and use), and the personal books of youngsters are all potential sources and suppliers of books. Basal and supplementary readers may also be among the books used. A constant flow of reading materials from many sources will offer the child a rich assortment of reading materials.

Reading Tradebooks

The teacher needs to become "drenched" in tradebooks if they are to be used most advantageously with youngsters in the course of an individualized reading program. The biggest and the hardest step to take is the first step. After the initial reading dosage, time devoted daily to reading tradebooks and the readings and sharings of the youngsters will be a continual source of replenishment for the teacher. He will be continually adding to his tradebook repertoire.

As the teacher reads more and more books, he will need to devise some method for "remembering" those books. A card file may be helpful. On one side of an index card, notations about the book can be made. On the other side of the card are questions which might be asked about the book. Through the course of the individualized reading program, as youngsters read these same books, they could submit questions to be added to these cards, or questions they feel would be "better" for their peers.

There are, of course, alternative methods. For example, the teacher may wish to structure his written comments so that they follow the line of questioning he plans for the conference time (with modifications made in the conference as he deems wise for various youngsters). This approach is discussed more fully in the section dealing with the conference time.

Each specific book card might provide a short summary of the book, plus questions to bring out the child's understanding of the content and to help him relate that content to his own experience and life. There may even be two or three notes on special aspects of the book, or the author, or the illustrator. There may be suggested activities related to the book, including skill activities. If there are particularly colorful words or words that build pictures, these, too, may be noted.

A creative teacher will, in the course of time, develop his own unique method of building his repertoire of books.

Testing and Diagnosing

The teacher will need to determine the youngster's reading level just as he would with any reading program. And when achievement level, oral reading realities, and interests are profiled, then it becomes necessary to have the supply of books to be commensurate with the reading levels and interests in that classroom.

How Many and Which Ones?

Preplanning includes the decision as to how many youngsters to begin with. While the teacher may feel secure enough to start with the total class, it may be easier to start with just a few children and work slowly until the whole group is reading under this plan of organization. Whatever the final decision for getting started, the teacher and the youngsters must feel at ease with the plan of organization. The teacher must do what he feels "right" for himself and for his youngsters. There is no one way.

Communication with Parents and Children

Parents should be apprised of the concept and intent of individualized reading. If they understand the program, they can support and reinforce the learnings and attitudes of the youngsters in the home. Parents can be a considerable help throughout the year by contributing books they have taken from the library on their own cards, books they have at home, and new books they have bought for the class. If the communication regarding the reading program is done in a manner that allows parents to ask questions, fears can be eased, and clear understandings may be the result.

Youngsters, too, need to be oriented to the program. The teacher explains that the children will select books that they want to read and that they will read at their own rate. There will be ample time to browse before selecting. He explains that the books are to be tradebooks alone, or tradebooks along with basal readers if that has been his decision. He tells them that they will be reading with the teacher, but that it will be in a special conference just between the teacher and the child, with grouping situations occurring intermittently.

It should be explained that they will be reading in groups at times but that the groups will be of a different nature. Sometimes they will read in interest groups, sometimes they will join a group that is planning a special project, and sometimes they will be with other children who need help with a particular skill. It should also be explained that there will be times when they may be in more than one group at a time. They should be made aware that groups are formed for a specific purpose and then disbanded when that purpose has been accomplished. A child may participate in a group session with several other youngsters who need instruction on a special skill; he may be reading with others who share his interest in a particular genre, such as historical fiction; he may be reading with those who share his regard for a specific author; he may be reading with those who are particularly enthusiastic about "horse" stories; he may be working with a group on a special project, such as a puppet show or a mobile; and he may be reading with his friends just for fun and pure enjoyment. All of these grouping situations have a place in the individualized reading program.

If youngsters are to keep a reading log, the teacher talks about the purposes and the use of it and gives them opportunities to add their suggestions. The teacher explains that each child is to maintain his own reading log for the purpose of entering the name of each book he has read, writing comments about the book, listing special words he wants to remember, noting questions he wants to bring up during his conference, listing suggestions for follow-up activities, and for listing the name of someone else who might like to read the book.

During the actual reading, he may have received help from someone, but he should still note the words that caused him to stop. He may wish to note a special part of the story that he wants to share with the teacher or with other youngsters. Noting page numbers in the book that he has prepared for reading aloud to the teacher, figurative language on certain pages, a favorite line, are a few suggestions. The log should be kept simple, with quality and not quantity being the major concern. And there may be times when notations will not be entered. Comments on each book may not be necessary. Whatever the plan for record keeping on the part of the youngsters, it should be explained thoroughly.

The teacher may need to introduce youngsters to the "rule of thumb" method of selecting books. When he finds a book that interests him, the youngster turns to the middle of the book and reads to himself. Each time he misses a word, he raises one finger. If he gets as far as his thumb on that one page, the book is probably too difficult for him, and he can put it aside for the time being and choose another one. This "rule of thumb" may not work with all youngsters, and the teacher may need to help some youngsters find a suitable book.

Each part of the plan of organization must be introduced carefully so that the youngsters are not confused or insecure. And always, there must be ample time for their questions and even more time for the answers to those questions.

Record Keeping[8]

The preplanning includes the teacher's decision as to his own unique method for record keeping. He will need to maintain a record of each

8. Barbe and Veatch resources give excellent ideas for keeping records for an Individualized Reading Program.

child's progress and needs from conference to conference. He will want to record the dates of each child's conferences, what he is reading, special words with which he needed help, and more.

The conference reveals what the child needs to learn in order to become a more skillful and fluent reader. By listening to the child's oral reading and by careful attention to his responses to questions, the teacher will diagnose word analysis, comprehension, interpretative, and critical reading needs.

The record may be a simple format wherein the teacher writes specifics and details. Or, it may be detailed and specific in format wherein he checks various items. For the former, there may be a loose-leaf notebook with several categories under which he would make notations: oral reading; perception or word attack skills; comprehension; interpretation; critical reading skills; comments and follow-up suggestions. For the latter, he might use a checklist for making notations of strengths and weaknesses. The teacher decides upon the format with which he would be most comfortable. There is no one way.

Reading manuals, as well as the Gray,[9] Barbe,[10] and Veatch[11] resources are helpful guides to the systematic presentation of the skills related to the reading process. The Taxonomy of Literary Understandings and Skills by Huck and Kuhn[12] could not be excelled as a means of giving the teacher a lucid delineation of those skills. Through consulting all these sources, and more, the teacher will devise his own unique method which will allow him to be concerned with the totality of skills and understandings. At all costs, the child's needs must be dealt with developmentally. This necessitates record keeping of a functional nature. The notes made during the conference time are used to direct future instruction.

Independent Activities

There is no dearth of creative independent activities which can spring from books. These activities may be group or individual endeavors. As the reading program progresses, youngsters will continually be a source of ideas themselves. To begin with, consider the following:

1. Bulletin boards of favorite characters or scenes
2. Creative writing

9. Gray, *On Their Own in Reading.*
10. Barbe, *Educator's Guide in Personalized Reading Instruction.*
11. Veatch, *Reading in the Elementary School.*
12. Charlotte S. Huck, and Doris Young Kuhn, *Children's Literature in the Elementary School,* 2d ed. (New York: Holt, Rinehart & Winston, 1968). See Appendix for the Taxonomy.

3. Book reviews
4. Dioramas
5. Box movies
6. Masks or other accompaniments for creative dramatics
7. Puppets
8. Games
9. Riddles
10. Puzzles

It is hoped that the first independent activity would be for the youngster to read his self-selected book, and after that, there should be creative use of time. That time will be "special" in the eyes of the youngster because it will represent a personal commitment. It is incumbent upon the teacher to insure a large block of time for uninterrupted silent reading.

Getting the Program Underway:
Selecting Books and Moving into the Conference

When the preliminary steps have been fulfilled to the teacher's satisfaction, then the day comes when the Individualized Reading Program gets underway.

A few children at a time should come to the library and browse. They may, at first, need help in selecting their books and finding one that is just right. They may need help in locating the books (there are different organizational procedures), in following the "rule of thumb," and in signing out the books of their choice.

In the selecting process, it would seem imperative to allow youngsters to take their time. This important phase of the program should not be rushed. If one keeps one's goals in mind, one will not be hurried. It is also imperative that, in the beginning stages of an individualized reading program, the teacher free himself to be available at this "browsing and selecting" time to give help and encouragement as it is needed.

Self-selection does not mean that children have complete freedom or independence of choice. Simply bringing an individual and a pile of books together does not insure results desired. Children need constant guidance in their choices of reading matter.

The principle of individualized reading does not imply that the teacher abandon his guidance or supervisory function toward children's reading. Teachers must continue to help the reader find satisfying experiences in keeping with his interests, purposes, and ability all at the same time. The teacher continues to play a significant role in stimulating and shaping these interests and purposes, and in helping the child evaluate realistically his abilities.

The teacher needs to decide how youngsters should sign up for a conference. Some teachers prefer to start out by assigning conference times for all the children. Later, conference times become voluntary, the children signing up on a special paper or on the chalkboard when they are ready. As the program progresses, the teacher's records will indicate if youngsters have been "skipping" conferences over a too-long period of time.

It will take several days to get all of the youngsters (whether we are talking about seven or thirty-five) settled with a self-selected book and by that time, one or two children will be ready for a conference.

As was stated earlier, the conference is the time when a youngster puts his best foot forward. By the same token, it is the time when the teacher, too, puts his best foot forward. Skillful, planned questioning is necessary if teachers are to help youngsters grow in literary understanding and skills.

As youngsters interact with stories, the responses should indicate development in levels of progress and growth. This means that the questions from the teacher should help youngsters move from literal to interpretative and critical levels of reading, reflecting, and responding. Naming and describing main characters, describing or summarizing the story, and reading aloud most exciting sentences or paragraphs cannot be the steady diet of questions dealing with stories. Questions should help youngsters form a gestalt and should give them an increasing awareness of the introduction, plot, and conclusion of stories.

The outline below is merely suggestive. The questions in parentheses could be directed to youngsters during the conference time. At times, the questions might be directed to them prior to conference time so that when they come to conference, they are ready to respond. The outline may be used for written reports later. It may also be used by the teacher as he reads and records his comments about tradebooks.

INTRODUCTION
   Characters in the story (Who are the most important people
      in this story?)
   Place (Where does most of the story take place?)
   Time (Is it a story about today's living, pioneer days . . .?)
PLOT
   Events leading up to climax (Tell about the most interesting
      and exciting part of the story.)
   Actual climax

ENDING OR CONCLUSION

Events happening after the climax (How does this story end?
What happens to the main character(s) in the story?)

At another level of development, youngsters could be asked to compare two of the main characters in appearance, personality, and anything else that would illustrate likenesses and differences of the two main characters.

A subsequent level of development could focus on the theme, that is, the author's purpose in writing the book, or story. A theme may be about love, or faith, or courage. Laura Ingalls Wilder's books show love and how close family relationships help overcome much hardship. Armstrong Sperry writes about bravery through the actions of Mafatu in *Call It Courage*.[13] Ask the children: "What purpose did the author have when he wrote the book you have just read? In other words, what is the theme of the book?"

Following that level, youngsters could be asked to compare the themes of two books. They would consider such thoughts as: (a) Is one more universal than the other? (b) Will both themes last through many years? Why, or why not? (c) Did each author develop his theme in an interesting and exciting way? (d) Explain the answer, using the development of the characters, plot, or . . .

And at still another level of development, two books could be compared, using any of these as means of comparison: (a) the main characters; (b) the era or time; (c) the readability; and (d) the genre or category.

Questions should help the child reach beyond simple literal comprehension to the complex process of interpretative and critical reading. He should begin to identify different types of literature and to evaluate the different types in terms of established criteria.[14]

As the child's reading increases, he will be able to make comparisons. He can compare a book of historical fiction with the factual material he is reading about that historical period. Some books may be read for comparison with a book on the same subject by another author. Some books are read to verify what has been written in another context. And some books are read for sheer enjoyment of the literary quality.

Some questions should offer the child the opportunity to suggest alternatives. These alternatives may be a change in the plot, a change in a character, a consideration of a different era and place, and a change in the ending of the story. Some of the questions should encourage the

13. Armstrong Sperry, *Call It Courage* (New York: Macmillan Co., 1941).
14. Criteria for evaluation of tradebooks are listed in the Appendix.

child to withhold judgment until he gathers more evidence for his opinions. He needs to grow in accepting the fact that opinions differ, that opinions can be challenged, but that opinions are valuable. He needs to look less and less for unconditional absolutes. Healthy skepticism and an open mind are needed.

For some questions, there are no "correct" answers. The answer a child gives is his own interpretation and his own personal response to what he has read. And some questions should help him apply what he has read to his own life and living.

The questioning, though, should not drain the enthusiasm of the child. If he doesn't enjoy it, he won't read. And if he doesn't read, we shall not have realized our primary goal.

The conference should be a time of enthusiastic exchange of thoughts, and of planning. The child knows that he and the teacher will determine just what comes next in his learning. He knows that he will receive instruction, either individually or with a group. He has confidence that his skills will increase and that his capacity for learning will be fulfilled. And he knows that the conference is a time when he will have an active part in that fulfillment.

The Classroom Library

No matter what the reading program may be, basal, individualized, or whatever, each classroom should have a planned book center, a classroom library.

The arrangement of the classroom library depends upon the seating arrangement in the room, the availability of book shelves, and the amount of extra furniture in the room. It is helpful if the teacher can obtain extra chairs for this center. The center should be an attractive and inviting nook, with a rug, pillows, a rocking chair and/or an easy chair. (The center is further discussed in Chapter 12.)

The arrangement of the books is to be determined by the teacher and the children. The children should be responsible for the orderliness of the library and should determine how the books are to be signed out, how they are to be kept in order. When children set the routines, they feel responsible for maintaining them. They will also determine how to record additional books that come to the class from book clubs, from special purchases, from parents, and from other sources.

The library should contain a variety of reading material. There will be tradebooks, basal reading books, paperbacks, reference books of all types, children's periodicals, magazines, newspapers, and the children's own original books.

Children should determine how the library is to be decorated. There can be a creative display area near or in the library. Some children may wish to feature each week one painting they like. Sometimes children like to highlight the area with clay models, puppets, or stuffed animals they have made. There may be a diorama to be set on the shelf or a wall-hanging of a favorite book. The appearance of the library and the classroom should reflect the interests, attitudes, and activities of the teacher and the children in working partnership as they interact with children's books.

Appendix 6 includes an extensive list of tradebooks suitable for individualized reading and the classroom library.

chapter 5

written expression

To teach children to write well and to enjoy writing is one of the major concerns of elementary teachers. In a very simple manner, teachers explain to youngsters that a writer's quest and contribution is to say in his own words what life has said to him; to say what he has felt, what he has experienced.

Creative writing is communicating things the writer knows very well—experiences he has had. He tries to make other people see and feel and realize what he has seen, felt, and realized. He tries to say something—not the way other people before him have said it—but the way he felt and experienced it. For example, how he felt the first day of spring when it was warm enough to go without heavy clothing. Or, how he felt on a very snowy day. And in the communicating, he tries to express himself so clearly—so vividly—as though he were saying something for the very first time to someone who really didn't know anything about these things at all.

Invigorating vocabulary expansion should accompany growth in written expression. When writing, one must strive all the time to find the exact word to use. Words are like tools. Each word, as each tool, has a particular job to do and is selected because the writer believes it can do that job better than any other tool. If a person wants to shovel snow off the walk, he doesn't go out with an ice pick in his hand. If he wants to sweep the floor, he doesn't use a rake. Words are the same way. And one of the excitements of writing is to find the exact word to say what one wants to say. Sometimes a writer hunts for a long time to find the right word, or words, for what he wants to say.

There is a spate of tradebooks to encourage written expression.

Summer Diary[1] is a book that hasn't as yet been written. The young vacationer or stay-at-homer is supposed to do that, fill in the blank pages

1. . . . (Owner), *Summer Diary*. Illustrated by Ruthven Tremain (New York: Macmillan Co., 1970). Ages 7 to 11.

as well as complete occasional sentences that read "My idea of a good time is to . . ."; "Tomorrow I shall . . ."; "Today I learned,—saw,—heard, —busted," and so forth. The owner of the book is to write the book from the beginning of June, or whenever his vacation starts, until school opens in September. There are interesting footnotes scattered throughout. For instance, this, under July 6: "In 1928, the largest hailstones ever—5.4 inches across, 17 inches around—fell on Potter, Nebraska." There is more: Under July 13, a definition of "triskaidekaphobia" (fear of the number 13); on July 23, a note about Charles Menches' inventing the ice cream cone in 1904; on August 7, a note on the inventor of the revolving door in 1888; and on the 9th of August, a note on the man who patented the escalator in 1859. And for the ocean bathers, this for August 18: In 1817 a sea serpent 100 feet long was seen undulating off the coast of Gloucester, Massachusetts. There are a lot of other things to catch the eye: a travel log, rainy day agenda, health reminders, two pages of self-adhering stickers to flag important events such as "I was stung by a bee," "haircut." Also, places are set aside for special jottings and things: snap-shots, doodles, the weather, a place to paste feathers and bubble gum wrappers, finances, books read ("comic books don't count"), addresses of old and new friends. It may be that the young diarist might come up with a better book of adventure and memories. He may decide on one for other months of the year, those of his own choosing. This diary is especially appropriate for children ages seven to eleven.

Walks for Children in San Francisco[2] is adapted from material first published in the San Francisco Chronical and is a useful and enticing book. Despite the faint whiff of travel brochure, it should appeal to young visitors to the city, since it is informal, informative, and organized for easy reference. General information is followed by separate units (two pages of text, two pages of easily-read maps) on geographic areas. A natural follow-up to reading this book would be to write another, *Walks for Children in (Buffalo, Columbus, East Lansing, Washington, D.C., etc.).*

In *Alphabet of Girls*[3] small girls and small boys, too, will be delighted by Leland Jacobs' verse which employs girls names to run gaily through the alphabet. And he doesn't skip a letter! What does he do with Q? Well—

2. Margot Patterson Doss, *Walks for Children in San Francisco.* Maps by Len Darwin (New York: Grove Press, 1969). Ages 9 to 11.
3. Leland B. Jacobs, *Alphabet of Girls.* Illustrated by John E. Johnson (New York: Holt, Rinehart & Winston, 1969). Ages 3 to 6.

> Queenie's strong and Queenie's tall.
> You should see her bat a ball,
> Ride a bike, or climb a wall.
> (Queenie's not her name at all.)

So goes the first of the three Queenie stanzas. For X, Jacobs says:

> She wishes her name was different,
> Like Caroline or Marie.
> But they named her for her Great Grandma,
> Whose name turned out to be:
> Xenobia.

Every child will agree with the last of these four stanzas:

> She is my friend—my special friend—
> The one I most prefer.
> She wishes her name was different
> And I agree with her—
> Xenobia.

For great fun with young listeners, open this attractively illustrated book anywhere and begin to read aloud. Creating an *Alphabet of Girls* or *An Alphabet of Boys* would be challenging to some youngsters. The boys could write the *Alphabet of Girls*, and the girls could do the same for one of the boys.

The best ways to build a good writing vocabulary are to read and write a good deal. Tradebooks offer incentives for doing both. However, even the titles of tradebooks are in themselves stimulators for written expression.

1. *The First and Last Animal Pet Parade*, Mary Neville. Illustrated by Jacqueline Chwast. New York: Pantheon Books, 1968. Ages 6-9.
2. *The Game*, Richard E. Drdek. Garden City, N. Y.: Doubleday & Co., 1968. Ages 10-14.
3. *The Day That Monday Ran Away*, Robert Heit. Illustrated by Joseph Veno. New York: Lion Press, 1969. Ages 7-10.
4. *A Trainfull of Strangers*, Eleanor Hull. Illustrated by Jean Sandin. New York: Atheneum Publishers, 1968. Ages 8-12.
5. *The Pool of Fire*, John Christopher. New York: Macmillan Co., 1968. Ages 11-16.
6. *The Hunkendenkens*, Richard R. Livingston. Illustrated by Harriet Pincus. New York: Harcourt, Brace & World, 1968. Ages 4-7.
7. *Spectacles*. Written and illustrated by Ellen Raskin. New York: Atheneum Publishers, 1968. Ages 4-8.

8. *Upside Down Day,* Julian Scheer. Illustrated by Kelly Oechsli. New York: Holiday House, 1968. Ages 3-6.
9. *The Museum House Ghosts,* Judith Spearing. Illustrated by Marvin Glass. New York: Atheneum Publishers, 1969. Ages 8-12.
10. *The Money Machine,* Keith Robertson. Illustrated by George Porter. New York: Viking Press, 1969. Ages 10-14.

All the titles listed in the "Oral Expression" section of this chapter are open invitations for creative writing, too.

There are other more well-known books which can aid and stimulate creative writing.

Charlie and the Chocolate Factory[4] is a popular fantasy. The assortment of children in the story is titillating—Augustus Gloop, a greedy fat pig of a boy; Veruca Salt, a spoiled, little rich girl whose parents always buy her what she wants; Violet Beauregarde, the world's champion gum chewer; Mike Teevee, a fresh child who spent every waking moment in front of the television set; and Charlie Bucket, the Hero, who was honest, brave, trustworthy, obedient, poor, and starving. One by one, the children are disobedient and meet with horrible accidents in the chocolate factory. Nothing, of course, happens to Charlie. Charlie is the future owner of the factory. But what if "The Factory Ran Out of Chocolate One Day!"

Pippi Longstocking[5] is a Swedish import. Pippi is an orphan who lives alone with her monkey and her horse in a child's utopian world in which she tells herself when to go to bed and when to get up. She has magical powers, and her so-called "logical thinking" delights eight-nine- and ten-year-olds. She does not attend school (except for one hilarious day), and she shocks adults with all that she does. But youngsters envy her, envy her, envy her. A pet horse and a pet monkey have prominent roles in Pippi's life. What would happen if there were a new pet? What difference would it make in Pippi's life? What bearing would it have on her pet horse and monkey? "A New Pet Arrives."

In *Whistle for Willie,*[6] Keats has captured a small boy's delight in learning how to whistle. But what if Peter woke up one morning and could not whistle for Willie, the dog? "The Day Peter Could Not Whistle for Willie!"

4. Ronald Dahl, *Charlie and the Chocolate Factory.* Illustrated by Joseph Schindelman (New York: Alfred A. Knopf, 1964).
5. Astrid Lindgren, *Pippi Longstocking.* Translated from the Swedish by Florence Lamborn. Illustrated by Louis S. Glanzman (New York: Viking Press, 1950).
6. Ezra Jack Keats, *Whistle for Willie* (New York: Viking Press, 1964).

In *When I Am Big*,[7] the frustrations of parental controls are depicted. Robert Paul Smith describes a small boy who looks forward eagerly to the time when he will be the one to pick up pieces of broken glass, insert plugs into sockets, and climb ladders to put up the storm windows. What would boys have to say if they wrote of that time in the future "When I Am Big"?

In the book *Someday*,[8] by Zolotow, some oft-dreamed-of wishes appear. For example, one double-page spread shows a little girl's dream as she practices the piano and says, "Someday . . . the lady across the street will call and say 'Please play that beautiful piece again'." Boys and girls of all ages will have unique thoughts to put in their "Someday" book.

In *Maurice's Room*,[9] Paula Fox has created a young hero who is more than a worthy antagonist in the conflict between children and grownups. Maurice and his friend, Jacob, are the only ones who know how to walk around Maurice's room. It is so filled (with what Mr. and Mrs. Henry insist on calling "junk") that at least once a month there is talk of moving to the country. There is also talk about Maurice finding new interests. But what could be more interesting than dead beetles, salamanders, tar balls, coffee cans, cigar boxes, or dried octopus? Dogs, hamsters, stuffed bears . . . and more? A natural title for creative writing: "My Room." Or, turn the tables so that boys are writing about "My Sister's Room," and girls are writing about "My Brother's Room."

Hobby Collections A-Z.[10] Almost everyone collects things, either on purpose or because he hates to throw something away. Any youngster with a hobby would know that topic intimately enough to write about "My Hobby Collection: S."

In *Professor Diggins' Dragons*,[11] a vacation that begins like any other turns into a real adventure when Mary Abby, John, Jarmes, Orson, and Lydia discover that dragons *do* exist, even today. And when Professor Diggins has ideas about how to pursue them, more surprises follow in this wise and delightful novel. In this story, dragons are one's

7. Robert Paul Smith, *When I Am Big.* Illustrated by Lillian Hoban (New York: Harper & Row, Publishers, 1965).
8. Charlotte Zolotow, *Someday.* Illustrated by Arnold Lobel (New York: Harper & Row, Publishers, 1964).
9. Paula Fox, *Maurice's Room.* Illustrated by Ingrid Fetz (New York: Macmillan Co., 1966).
10. Roslyn W. Salny, *Hobby Collections A-Z.* Illustrated by Robert Galster (New York: Crowell, Collier & Macmillan, 1965).
11. Felice Holman, *Professor Diggins' Dragons.* Illustrated by Ib Ohlsson (New York: Macmillan Co., 1966).

fears. Creative writing could stem from "My Dragon and How I Overcame It" or "My Dragon and What I Am Doing to Overcome It."

The Red Balloon[12] by the late Lamorisse is replete with creative writing themes. The balloon could be personified in parts of the story. For example, "The Balloon Speaks," or "The Balloon Tries to Go to School." Having heard the story, the youngsters could change the ending. Before youngsters read the sequel, *The Trip in the Balloon,* have them write their own sequel. The final illustration (photograph) would be a motivator for that title.

Anatole,[13] by Eve Titus, is a cheese-tasting mouse who is as French as his little beret and bicycle. He saves M'sieur Duval's cheese factory from financial ruin and becomes First Vice-President in charge of cheese-tasting! Other books tell of further adventures of this resourceful French mouse. What would happen if this very-French mouse found himself in a strange foreign country? "Anatole in the United States" is a title that should elicit interesting narrations from youngsters.

Happiness Is a Warm Puppy[14] and *Security Is a Thumb and a Blanket,* by Schulz, are open invitations for youngsters to write what happiness and security mean to them.

Different beginnings, different endings, changing characters, changing the locale of the story, personification of animals and the inanimate, autobiographies, expressing how illustrations make one feel—these and many other written expressions should find a place in the language arts program.

Tradebooks can enrich written expression in still other ways.

No young person who is interested in writing will want to miss *Someday You'll Write*[15] by Elizabeth Yates. This brief but comprehensive guide to the art and craft of good writing, written by the author of *Amos Fortune, Free Man,* is perceptive, sensitive, and eminently sensible. The book discusses writing from the point of view of the creative writer. Miss Yates explains how the writer chooses his subject, develops the narrative, keeps the reader interested, disciplines himself so that he becomes a craftsman and is not afraid of hard work—because writing is hard work. Miss Yates states, "Have something to say and stop when you have said it." The book was written when an eleven-year-old explained that she wanted to know how books were written

12. Albert Lamorisrse, *The Red Balloon* (Garden City, N. Y.: Doubleday & Co., 1956). Also, *Trip in a Balloon.*

13. Eve Titus, *Anatole.* Illustrated by Paul Galdone (New York: McGraw-Hill Book Co., 1956).

14. Charles M. Schultz, *Happiness Is a Warm Puppy* (San Francisco: Determined Productions, 1962).

15. Elizabeth Yates, *Someday You'll Write* (New York: E. P. Dutton & Co., 1962).

and how a person got to be a writer. Chapter titles include "How to select a subject"; "How to start with an interesting beginning and how to make an ending come gradually"; How to continue—but not too far —and keep your reader interested"; "Something about a story that is True"; "And now—to write"; "Discipline that delights"; and "Salute to a fellow craftsman."

The *First Book of Creative Writing*[16] is more routine in presentation than Yates's *Someday You'll Write*. Written by Julia C. Mahon and illustrated by Gustave E. Nebel, the book is appropriate for grades five to eight. It is an introductory guide to the fundamentals of good writing. The author defines creative writing, describes and gives an example of a composition, a book report, and a short story, and discusses the mechanics of plotting, characterization, setting, grammar, style, and word usage. In conclusion, she gives brief attention to the development of habits of observation and the use of libraries.

See Yourself in Print: A Handbook for Young Writers[17] is based on the assumption that almost everyone can write for profit. This brisk, breezy guide to writing and marketing of articles, stories, and fillers offers both motivational stimulation and practical advice. The author describes various types of marketable writing, gives suggestions on the selection of markets and the preparation of manuscripts, and discusses techniques of writing fiction and non-fiction in relation to content and audience appeal. She illustrates her remarks with numerous examples drawn mainly from her own works. The lively pen-and-ink drawings tend to emphasize feminine appeal, but the sound, well-balanced advice should prove useful to writers of both sexes in grades six and up.

How to Write a Report[18] offers practical suggestions for gathering and organizing information and making written and oral reports. The major portion of the book deals with such basic skills as using reference books, making notes, compiling bibliographies, and making outlines. A final section discusses briefly various ways of recording information about books and different types of oral and written book reports. Clear explanations supplemented by examples make the book especially useful for upper-grade classes in elementary schools.

Letter writing is writen expression that can be "sparkly" or dull. It all depends.

16. Julia C. Mahon, *First Book of Creative Writing*. Illustrated by Gustave E. Nebel (New York: Franklin Watts, 1968).
17. Nan Gilbert Hawthorn, *See Yourself in Print: A Handbook for Young Writers*. Illustrated by Jacqueline Tomes (New York: Hawthorn Books, 1968).
18. Sue R. Brandt, *How to Write a Report*. Illustrated by Peter P. Plasencia (New York: Franklin Watts, 1968).

Letter writing is a trial to many youngsters. Irrelevant purposes, letter-writing assignments lacking real motivation, the burdens of pressure and stress, and an ordeal that often culminates in a bitter ending —the "circular" file—are too often characteristic. It is no wonder children give up.

Children's literature gives impetus to honest letter-writing realities—real people with whom to communicate—the authors and illustrators—relevant, interesting, and honest questions to ask.

The following are some questions that might be asked of a few specific authors. The teacher will help youngsters wonder about more questions. Together, they will think of many more. The answers will delight even the most placid.

Maia Wojciechowska

To communicate with the author of the 1965 Newbery winner would be intriguing to all boys. *Shadow of a Bull* is very much related to a deep interest of that author.

1. Have you seen many bullfights?
2. How did you find out enough to write about bullfighting?
3. Why do you like to write about boys?
4. How did you get the idea for Manola?
5. Your writings contain courage of some kind. Is there a reason for this?
6. Did you ever fight a bull?
7. Did Manola become a famous doctor?
8. How long did it take you to write *Shadow of a Bull?*

Maia Wojciechowska has seen between 150 and 200 bullfights. She likes to write about boys because as a girl, she wanted so much to be a boy. And, she has indeed fought a bull. Need I say more about intriguing the boys?

Marguerite Henry

Marguerite Henry is one of the more skillful writers of horse stories. To listen to her is to learn always.

1. At what age did you begin writing, and why?
2. What makes you interested in writing about horses and animals rather than people?
3. Are the animals you write about really living?
4. Are the incidents in the stories based on real events?
5. In *Black Gold*, was Jadey, the jockey, a real person?
6. Where did you do your research for *All about Horses?*
7. When you are ready to start a new book, what is the first step?

The winner of the 1949 Newbery award, for *King of the Wind,* started her writing career at the age of eleven. She began writing to round out her life. She wanted to be strong physically and to excel in athletics. Instead she was skinny. Boys referred to her as "that tall-long-drink." She began writing to create strong characters who could do all the things that she could not do. Some of the animals in her stories are real and still living, or their descendents are still living. In *Black Gold*, almost all the incidents are based on real events. Black Gold really did win the Kentucky Derby, and he finished his last race on three legs. King of the Wind, the swift Arabian stallion, did become the great, great, great, grandsire of almost every superior thoroughbred on the track today.

Children will learn that Marguerite Henry is ubiquitous in her research. She does her research everywhere. In order to learn about prehistoric horses for *All about Horses*, she visited the Chicago Museum of Natural History where she studied the life-size models of the prehistoric animal right down to equus, the horse of today. And she spent much time in libraries reading books on history, anatomy, horse diseases, and so forth. She visited stables all across the United States to study at first hand the various breeds and how they differ. She interviewed veterinarians, horse owners, trainers, and breeders. She joined the American Horseshoers Association and talked to shoers to learn about horses' feet. This and much more will both awe and inspire youngsters.

Marguerite deAngeli

Different kinds of questions would go to authors who both write and illustrate.

1. Where do you get the ideas for your books? Do the ideas for your stories come from your pictures, or do the ideas for the pictures come from the stories?
2. Which do you prefer—writing or painting?
3. Do you learn the customs of the country you are writing about by visiting the country or by reading about it?
4. Did you go to Art School?
5. One notices that there are maps in the front of your books. Do you write the story first and then draw the map?
6. How did you feel when you won the John Newbery award?
7. Have you ever had any other jobs besides writing and painting?
8. Was there a particular school subject you were not good at?
9. Have you ever wanted anything as Shad wanted copper-toed boots?
10. As a little girl, did you ever long for something that you could not have?

The humanness of this wonderful person will come through in all her responses. For example, she says that, on hearing the news of the

award, her whole family just sat down and cried. She tells about a specific school subject she was not good at—arithmetic—and how lacking
that skill put an end to a very brief clerking career. There is fascination
behind every one of her books. Youngsters should be encouraged to
inquire as to how she came to write a book that had special interest
for them.

Eleanor Estes

The Moffats, The Middle Moffat, Rufus M., The Hundred Dresses
—these are but a few of the books by Eleanor Estes.

1. How did you happen to think about writing books like *The Moffats?*
2. Why do you for the most part write family books?
3. Are the characters your family?
4. What made you write *The Hundred Dresses?*
5. Is part of it real and part of it fictional? Which parts are which?
6. Why don't you write a book about what happened to Wanda as
   she grew up?
7. Why didn't you have Maddie stick up for Wanda in *The Hundred
   Dresses?*
8. In your book, *Rufus M.,* you said, "To Teddy." Who is Teddy?
9. Where do you get the different names for your characters?
10. Where did Pye come from?
11. Did you ever go to Fire Island off Long Island Sound?
12. Were you in Pinky Pye?
13. Did you have a New York cat named Gracie? A dog named Ginger?
    A kitten named Pinky Pye?

Youngsters will be fascinated with this information. For example,
The Hundred Dresses was based upon an event in the author's childhood. She has a realistic reason for not writing a sequel—one that would
bear remembering. And there will be information the children haven't
asked for, the "extras" that will come along with the answers. For example, it will titillate youngsters to learn that, long before the author
wrote the book, she wrote speeches at night accepting the Newbery
award.

There are at least four other bright letter-writing experiences. Pupils in one elementary school can get to know pupils in another elementary school (in the same school system or in a neighboring school
system) through written correspondence. Learning about each other's
book interests, about activities and hobbies resulting from books, could
result from an exchange of letters.

Corresponding with youngsters in other countries about books, authors, favorites in "our" country, and so forth can come about by se-
curing names of pen pals from YOUTH OF ALL NATIONS, 16 St.

Lukes' Place, New York, New York 10014. This would be especially significant in 1972 which has been designated as International Book Year. There would be other learnings, too, as they correspond with youngsters in other countries. For example, as they write to and hear from boys and girls in London, they would learn about the Children's Book Stores there. For, in London, children have bookstores of their own. Or, if youngsters were to write to youngsters in Ireland, they would learn that children in Ireland are fortunate enough to have traveling storytellers. The storyteller comes to the neighborhood and rings his bell to call the children to him—much as our ice cream vendors do in this country.

There is also the letter-writing and composing pupils will do if they correspond with youngsters in an International School regarding word origins and word study, as was mentioned earlier in this chapter. And last, but not least, I wish they would write to this author and let her know what they are discovering and learning about words, people, language, and books.

A Concluding Viewpoint Teachers need to believe that youngsters can write. They should help youngsters to know that they get ideas from many places—if they will keep their ears pricked and their eyes wide. Teachers need to provide time for writing. Ample time. Leisurely time. And throughout, young writers will need encouragement and understanding, whether they are struggling over the writing of one sentence, one paragraph, or a complete work.

The way to develop good writing is with good reading. Literature develops sensitivity to language, provides models for good writing in different forms, and may serve as a touchstone for creative writing. There must be scheduled time for youngsters to hear good literature. Children must be given a feeling for the sound and meaning of words, for the patterns of language by being read to often. Daily! By making certain that youngsters hear the finest literary quality and by discussing that literature, the teacher will have oportunities to point out and encourage the following in written expression:

1. Imagery—describing a situation or a subject in vivid, colorful, concrete language.
2. Naturalness—expressing one's individuality.
3. Inventiveness—inventing fresh characters, settings, plots, or words; playing with homonyms, alliteration.
4. Conciseness and Clarity—expressing the essence of an idea or situation; avoiding words and details which distract from the main ideas or impressions to be conveyed.
5. Flexible Style—avoiding monotony by altering sentence length, clause position, sentence type, and other elements of style.

For those who so desire, creative writing can be dictated. Use of a tape recorder should be permitted. Once his thoughts are on tape, the youngster may wish to transfer them to paper. For those who feel this is not in keeping with "high standards," let it be recalled that more than one prominent writer of children's books does just that. One famous biographer even dictates as she researches in libraries, in preference to writing. She finds that to write her notes takes away from the joy of it all and that it takes too much time. Instead, she "talks" her notes.

Once children have written, something should be done with their compositions. For example, they can be published in a book entitled *Young Writers of Room* . . . The publication should be made available on the school and neighborhood library shelves. Or, they can be published in another way. A new magazine, *Kids,* (Kids' Publishers, Inc.) probably offers the most realistic avenue for publication of the writings of youngsters. It is a magazine written by youngsters for each other.

A Writing Center in the classroom can be helpful. An extra desk, or table, can be set aside for this writing corner. Dictionaries of all kinds, reference books, and a raft of word books should be located here. At least one typewriter (and a manual of practice lessons to go with it) and a tape recorder should be made available. Typing not only makes the writing process go faster for some youngsters, but teachers have reported that youngsters who type their creative works tend to write at greater length and with more facility. Some who otherwise might not write are "moved" by the typewriter. All the tools of a writer should be located here. Paper, pencils, carbons, typewriter erasers, and so forth. The youngsters themselves can be responsible for the "upkeep," for example, sharpening the pencils so that they are ever-ready, and making sure there is an ample supply of paper from the supply room. Youngsters could be responsible for the planning and ongoing development of this writing center.

If need be, they can be given diaries or notebooks as incentives. Noting happenings, feelings, thoughts—all jottings for later "take-offs" —will help some boys and girls. Group composing and coauthors should be permitted. Collaboration is a reality in everyday life. Writing-illustrating teams should be encouraged, too. Sometimes, classroom editors ought to be provided—editors for spelling, grammar suggestions, and so on. (Once a writer has penned his thoughts, the editing may rightfully be the responsibility of someone other than the creator—much as it is in adult life.) Not always, though. Just sometimes.

Joy in written expression and excellence through reasonable control of mechanics are both goals to be sought. There is a time when the pupil's thoughts are all-important, and there is a time to place emphasis on the mechanics of writing. This is not to imply that one is important and the other is not. But, rather, it says that there is a time and place for each concern.

The thought. The thought with precision and grace.

chapter 6

listening

And everywhere there is listening! Youngsters listen to
—the story of Sir Nigel
—new words and meanings
—concepts unfolding
—the playback of their oral activities
—the interest groups in individualized reading
—the creative writings of their classmates
—choral speaking
—moods of poems
—sounds of words, poems, and stories
—literature, literature, literature.

For how will they ever love to read literature unless they first love to hear literature? The listening experiences should enhance the development of the many facets of literature. Then we will truly be providing for the total art.

There is another important reason for listening. Boys and girls need to hear the rhythm and pattern of language. They need to understand how we put thoughts into words. They need to understand that thoughts and words go together and form patterns. And that thoughts, words, patterns, make sentences. In order to understand this, they need to hear words, patterns, sentences, and they need to "make" thoughts into patterns and sentences.

The teacher may select a title of a tradebook and write it on the board. As youngsters respond to his requests about that title, he may write their responses on the board underneath the title being discussed. For example, *I Like Winter,* by Lois Lenski.

"Let's change 'I' to someone else."
  (Billy, Susie, Mommy, Daddy, he, she)

"Change 'Winter' to another time or to something else."
  (Summer, spring, fall, . . .)

50

"Change 'like'."

"Put something in front of 'winter' 'spring' 'summer'."
(or whatever the responses were) (cold winter, hot summer or whatever)

"Put something in front of 'like'."
(Don't like a cold winter)

Thus, youngsters become involved with transformational grammar. The teacher is showing them that they can "make" and "transform" as they take one simple sentence and change it, making it bigger (or smaller) with other titles. Youngsters are thus hearing and participating in the patterns of language. They are hearing and participating in the structure of language. What is important is that they are hearing the patterns as well as making the patterns. They are hearing structure as they transform and structure. But only a limited amount of time should be spent on study specific to grammar or usage. For instructional time can be spent to greater advantage in actually *using* the language both orally and in written forms; time can be spent to greater advantage in *hearing* and reading language.

A tape recorder with headsets is an extremely valuable tool for the classroom. It permits youngsters to hear fine writing over and over again. To read with discrimination and taste a pupil must first hear discriminating and tasteful literary works. Records and tapes permit him to listen as often as he desires.

The recordings may be commercial ones done by professionals and authors. Or they might be done by local storytellers, the teacher, and youngsters themselves. Recordings can be made of complete books, with music at the beginning of each chapter so that boys and girls may easily select specific chapters to hear. The music would get them ready to listen when the chapter begins. Youngsters should be allowed to decide which stories they want recorded. Their requests should be respected, for in many cases, this is the first time anyone has asked them what they would like to have recorded. The recording doesn't always have to be of a complete literary work. Youngsters' may wish to record their favorite passages or chapters for others to hear.

Hearing the patterns of language through literature will help youngsters when they themselves read. It will not be word-to-word reading, but rather they will read as one should read music. It will be the difference between the staccatoed-puncture of individual notes and the blend of a complete phrase. Sentence sounds and pattern sounds are more important than the individual word sounds.

Children should be given the feeling of language and literature. They should be led to feel it in their ears, to get it in their ears.

Listening is a large enterprise. Large in terms of time spent in listening during a school day, large in terms of the need for sharp and refined listening skills, and large in terms of opportunities for listening. All the small endeavors will contribute to the whole—to the total. All the little bits will add up. It might be well to begin with *The Tiniest Sound*,[1] a series of miniatures described in blank verse. Is the tiniest sound in the world made by fog, a milkweed seed falling on a lamb, kitten paws walking on fur, or . . .?

1. Mel Evans, *The Tiniest Sound* (Garden City, N. Y.: Doubleday & Co., 1969).

part
two

the sciences

chapter 7

the social studies

Concerned with a study of man and his relationship to his social and physical world, social studies adapts the content and methods of the various social sciences, either in terms of a particular discipline or through a cross-disciplinary approach, often enriched by ideas from the humanities and the natural sciences.

Objectives

There has been little research done concerning social studies education objectives, although many viewpoints have been expressed. The results of investigations by Bloom and Krathwohl[1] into the cognitive domain and by Krathwohl and others[2] into the affective domain have provided basic general taxonomies of educational objectives which leaders in social studies education have used in developing objectives that can be implemented and evaluated.

Organizing the Curriculum

"Significant trends in elementary school curriculum patterns include more emphasis in inquiry, human relationship, contemporary affairs, and cross-disciplinary social science. The unit method of teaching is preferred."[3]

A current trend in social sciences education is to design units of instruction that are based on concepts and generalizations drawn

1. Benjamin S. Bloom and David R. Krathwohl, *Taxonomy of Educational Objectives: Handbook I: The Cognitive Domain* (New York: David McKay Co., 1956).
2. David R. Krathwohl et al., *Taxonomy of Educational Objectives: Handbook II: The Affective Domain* (New York: David McKay Co., 1964).
3. J. R. Skretting and J. E. Sundeen, "Social Studies Education," in *Encyclopedia of Educational Research,* ed. Robert Ebel (New York: Macmillan Co., 1969).

from the social sciences. The intent is to provide opportunities for students to learn concepts and main ideas that are durable and of greatest importance in studying human relationships. The concepts and related content are taken from such fields as history, geography, economics, political science, anthropology, sociology, psychology, and philosophy.[4]

The Unit of Instruction and Its Initiation

A unit of instruction is a series of learning experiences focused upon the achievement of a common goal which pupils have accepted as their own.[5] Initiating the unit, carrying on research, involvement in a wide variety of activities, and culmination are usually phases in units of instruction. Tradebooks make a major contribution to each of these phases.

After the choice of the unit has been made, either within or without a framework of suggested units, the initiation is of major concern in order that the unit may get off to a good start. There are many ways of initiating a unit that have proved valuable. All of them must meet these criteria: arousing interest, raising questions and issues that demand research and further exploration, and providing a common experience from which to plan.

Arranging the environment, or providing a "setting" that will arouse interest on the part of the children, is one effective way to initiate a unit. An arranged environment includes an ample display of well-selected tradebooks.

As the children explore the environment and browse through the books on the reading table, any one child may bring a book to the teacher to ask about a picture, or to tell what he has read. The child may want to read and share this story or the description of the picture with the class. The teacher himself may bring to the sharing period a book that he knows will give the children a common experience from which to plan what they will do next. The teacher may select and use a short story or an excerpt from a longer story that includes many of the problems he hopes the children will want to study. During the discussion that follows the reading of the story, open-end questions should bring out these problems and issues so that the pupils identify themselves with the problem and see the need for additional research.

If the environment and the additional activities have been stimulating enough, children will identify many problems and issues around

4. John U. Michaelis, *Teaching Units in the Social Sciences* (Skokie, Ill.: Rand McNally & Co., 1968), p. 1.
5. Lavone A. Hanna, Gladys L. Potter, and Neva Hagaman, *Unit Teaching in the Elementary School* (New York: Holt, Rinehart & Winston, 1963), p. 139.

which the unit can be organized. While this is being done, the pupils may be reading various tradebooks that further illustrate or enlarge upon the problems they stated.

Selected tradebooks are introduced during the initiatory period—those books which will serve the purpose of the initiation. The use of additional tradebooks throughout the unit is necessary because of their vital role in the development and success of a unit.

Research Experiences in the Unit

Once the unit has been initiated, children are ready to search for answers to the questions and problems that have been generated in the exploratory period. The heart of unit study is research. Young adults gain information from field trips, resource people, audiovisual aids, magazines, newspapers, textbooks, and tradebooks.

Accurate information and additional knowledge about the subject at hand will be needed continuously by children throughout the development of a unit. As children decide to make objects, they will need to go to many books, audiovisual aids, and other sources in order to discover the kind or type of things to be made, their uses, and directions for making them.

Research in the first and second grades is of necessity very simple. Children gather their information from watching films, from listening to the teacher tell or read a story, from doing a simple experiment, from going on trips, by talking with adults, from viewing pictures and slides, and from reading simple charts or books. The amount of research that children in grades three to eight can and should do will continually increase.

Research Through the Use of Reading Materials

Reading is an integral part of almost every experience children have as their units develop. Research, construction, experiments, searching for the music of an era almost always require reading. And that reading should extend beyond textbooks. Tradebooks will often give more current information. And the large number of tradebooks available on all topics makes the accommodating of reading abilities a greater likelihood. The tradebooks available need to extend beyond the informational genre. For example, stories, poems, folktales, and biographies help children gain a feeling for the people about whom they are studying as well as an understanding of their way of life. Locational skills, like word-study skills, are used continuously as children use multiple books, library facilities, maps, globes, and charts.

The teacher should plan for the research period as carefully as he would plan for any other experience. Problems that the children are likely to encounter should be anticipated. New and difficult words and concepts should be noted so that they can be explained. A wide range of reading materials should be included in order to meet the span of reading abilities in a classroom. For example, a sixth grade class might have children whose reading level varies from grades 2.4 to 11.6. They would need reading materials that range from the second to the eleventh grade if the slow readers are to succeed and the accelerated readers are to be challenged. The higher the grade, the wider is the range in reading abilities.

In the primary grades, the teacher, in gathering material for the children to read, may slip a piece of paper into the books to show where the specific information can be located, or he may put the page references on the chalkboard. Children will need to know where in the room library shelves for the specific books for their particular committees may be found. As children mature, they will become more independent in the use of reference materials, and they should be able to locate information by using the index or the table of contents.

Children at all ages will need help and guidance from the teacher during the research period if it is to be successful. In planning with the children, it is helpful to have them review the questions for which they are seeking answers. The teacher will want to be certain that individual youngsters are aware of the questions for which they are responsible. He needs also to help the pupils review the work-study skills they have learned: where to find the index, how to use books and reference materials, what type of notes to take, and how to make simple outlines. It is well to agree upon the behavior expected of children before they start to work. These might include the following:

—To use the table of contents, the index, and the appendix
—To complete the pertinent materials in one book before reading another
—To take simple notes
—To put the information in their own words
—To check the accuracy of their information
—To note the date of publication of book, newspaper, or magazine
—To gather the data they have agreed to research for their committee
—To validate information by giving the title of the book and author.

In carrying out the tasks, the class may be organized into as many working groups as seems desirable. Some children could work alone, some in pairs, and others in committees. The teacher may need to take some children to a table or form a group to give them additional help. This may be done by having the children with reading difficulties look at picture books and read a selected paragraph or two; or the teacher may read pages to them and discuss the pertinent information contained in the selection. This information may then be recorded by a member of the group for the committee report.

With the number of excellent tradebooks available and with the wide ranges in reading ability that are present in every classroom, pupils in the elementary school should have many books and reference materials for research work. The use of a single textbook greatly cripples children in their ability to use work-study skills. It is desirable that pupils begin to have more than one author's viewpoint, that they learn that a single book very often cannot contain all the needed information, and that more than one book is needed for a comprehensive picture. The bibliography suggests tradebooks for the social studies.

Research Through the Use of Nonprint Materials

Research may be carried on through a variety of resources other than books. Information can be acquired when children take a study trip; listen to a report, the radio, or a visitor; see a motion picture, a filmstrip, or slides; interview someone; perform an experiment; study pictures, maps, globes; or watch television. A combination of print and nonprint materials is usually needed for the best results.

Resource people. Many different kinds of persons are valuable sources of information for children throughout the grades. Resource people can verify information youngsters have secured in their research, and children can be assisted in evaluating the tradebooks they have read. For example, an auto mechanic visiting a classroom could be requested to look at the tradebook sources in the classroom and indicate which sources are the most valid in view of his unique experiences and expertise.

Audiovisual Aids. Audiovisual materials include many worthwhile aids to learning. There are maps and globes, motion pictures, recordings, slides, filmstrips, study prints, models, artifacts, graphs, charts, exhibits, radio, and television. These aids are particularly valuable in making past events and distant people come alive for children, in giving color and drama to the pages of a book, and in giving concreteness to abstract concepts and ideas. Audiovisual materials can be compared to information found in tradebooks and can be used to interpret, clarify, and extend that information. The use of audiovisual materials and tradebooks go hand in hand. Together they foster critical reading and critical thinking.

Models and Real Objects. Children have a difficult time visualizing things that they have never seen. Objects and models can give them accurate understanding which would otherwise be impossible. The artifacts of other cultures—weapons, utensils, tools, clothing, ornaments, jewelry, pottery, clocks, musical instruments, and art objects—take on new meaning when children can see and handle them. Models of ships, covered wagons, buildings, furniture, and dolls dressed in authentic costumes arouse interest and deepen understandings.

In introducing a unit of work, a teacher will attempt to have as much realia, or real things, in the room as possible. These are introduced to arouse the children's curiosity and their interest as to what the objects are, how they are or were used, why, and when. Often, youngsters want to make objects; they do research in tradebooks in order to find out how.

Children can learn to refer to pictures in tradebooks time after time for accurate details, for clues about making things, for information about clothing that people wore or about utensils and tools they used. Edwin Tunis, Miroslav Sasek, and Isaac Asimov are particularly helpful to the intermediate grades in their detailed graphics related to models, objects, and the life of other eras and other places (see bibliography).

Study Trips. The purposes of study trips are to motivate interest, to gather information, to correct erroneous concepts and false information, and to provide sensory impressions that will help develop clear concepts. After the trip, children may wish to return to tradebook illustrations which will now take on added and new meaning. Information read before the trip will now be viewed critically for verification, rejection, or further researching.

Activities

From a comprehensive point of view, everything that is done by the teacher and the children in the development of a unit comes under the heading of activities. With this interpretation, activities include planning, organizing purposes and procedures, carrying on research, working with data, sharing what has been learned, and evaluating. In this section, however, the discussion of activities will be directed toward those things which the children do with the information that they have gathered through their extensive research.

The purpose of such activities is to help children organize, clarify, understand, and assimilate their data. Activities infuse data with life. Since these activities use information youngsters have gathered through research, it follows that usually the activities can be organized and initiated only after the greater part of the research is under way. Research should not assume a minor role.

After the children have collected considerable data through organized research, they are ready to use their information in various activities. Most units involve, potentially, activities within each of the following interrelated categories: (1) socially significant work; (2) collections and exhibits; (3) experiments; (4) dramatization; (5) construction; and (6) aesthetics. Tradebooks furnish information for collecting and exhibiting; they give ideas and procedures for art and construction activities, materials and steps for experiments; they offer suggestions for dramatization; and they indicate music related to eras and countries being studied. Neither the tradebooks nor the activities are exhaustive in coverage. Space limitations of this book necessitate only a brief look at suggestions. In the discussion that follows, there will be no specification of unit topics from which the activities might emanate. Many of the activities would relate to more than one unit topic, and those topics will be evident to the reader as he considers the activities.

Collections and Exhibits

Children profit by and enjoy collecting and assembling materials that contribute to units of instruction. Activities of this type provide children with experiences in the organization of data. If a child, for example, is arranging an exhibit of spices of various sorts, he needs to differentiate among the various kinds. Children are natural collectors and should be encouraged in this rich firsthand experience.

Museums and local business establishments offer collections and exhibits for youngsters to view; for example, artifacts, stones, utensils and tools from pioneer days, and coins. However, youngsters need to do more than merely view—they need to become involved themselves in collecting. They may collect and exhibit building materials as they study shelter. They may collect realia and clothing in a unit on Mexico or models as they study transportation and equipment as they study communication.

Tradebooks offer up-to-date information and guidelines to collecting. For example, *Hobby Collections A-Z*[6] is a complete guide to col-

6. Roslyn W. Salny, *Hobby Collections A-Z* (New York: T. Y. Crowell, 1966).

lecting and exhibiting. There are many techniques for organizing a collection. For each type of collection, the professional methods of organizing and displaying are discussed.

While the latter tradebook gives a view of many collections, there are tradebooks about specific collections, for example, *The Story of Israel in Stamps.*[7] The beautiful and exciting stamps issued by Israel since 1948 tell her story in dramatically graphic terms. Actually, the wide variety of topic specialities makes stamp collecting a natural and informative parallel for many units.

The Story of Coins[8] is an introduction to numismatics. The book outlines the beginnings of money, from barter through ancient Greek and Roman coins; it describes modern minting methods; it tells how to start a coin collection and how to store and display the coins; it traces the history of American coins; and it identifies official coins of the United States. The book also includes information on mint marks and key or "controller" coins, and it contains a glossary, a bibliography, and a photo index of coins and odd money in addition to the regular index. The illustrations are profuse.

From agate and amber to zinc and zircon, *Rocks and Rock Collecting*[9] offers advice on tools necessary for rock collecting, and on locating, identifying, mounting, and swapping rock specimens.

All activities should be learning experiences. There must be relationships between collecting activities and the understandings to be developed. The intent here is not to treat activities as though there should be no relationships. Each activity must be related to main ideas, concepts, and questions. For example, in studying the origin of the United States and Canada, children could secure various samples of materials that were sought in early explorations. Samples of various spices might be collected. With such an activity, boys and girls could see, touch, smell, and taste. This experience of collecting spices would relate to the main idea that significant contributions were made by many countries through their explorations. The concepts to be developed would be:

1. We study history to understand the past better and to plan for improvement in the future.
2. Cultures are changed by discovery and exploration.

7. G. Shamir, *The Story of Israel in Stamps* (New York: Funk & Wagnalls, 1969). Ages 8-up.
8. Sam Rosenfeld, *The Story of Coins.* Illustrated by James Barry (Irrington-on-Hudson, N. Y.: Harvey House, 1968). Ages 9-up.
9. Eva Knox Evans, *Rocks and Rock Collecting* (Racine, Wis.: Golden Press, 1970). Ages 8-up.

3. Individuals are affected by their cultural backgrounds, and in turn, influence and modify any new group contacted.

Of course, no one learning experience or activity will develop all the concepts. And *Everything Nice, The Story of Sugar and Spice*[10] is one highly informative book on the subject of spices and includes simple recipes.

Although collecting may begin as a learning experience related to a unit of instruction, the activity can become a hobby. Collections thus often lead to rewarding lifetime habits.

Experimentation

Through experimentation, children are testing the accuracy of their information. They have collected data, and they want to find out "if it really works that way." Children are taught to be critical of sources of information and to verify, or to reject data on the basis of the best evidence available. Some of the evidence may be obtained through experimentation. Experimentation would include the making of butter, bread, and the like. However, this discussion will focus on the more formal experiments of science.

The bibliography shows that there is no dearth of tradebooks which offer sugestions for experiments. The use of those tradebooks is the major concern of this discussion.

In criticizing the bookish approach to the development of experiments, Blough offers the following illustration:

> One child reads from the text the directions for performing the experiment; another child performs the experiment accordingly, and a third child reads from the book the results of the experiment.[11]

The use of tradebooks needs to involve much more than that. It is not so much the spirit of "reading from," but of testing the accuracy of that information. Youngsters have collected data, and they want to find out if it "really works that way." They should hold tentatively to what they have read, and they will obtain evidence through experimentation. More than "three" youngsters should be involved and in a manner different from that portrayed above.

Experiments should be replicated at times. Replication is necessary for several reasons. Sometimes the viewers "miss" a step, and this consequently "hazes" concept development. Sometimes the experi-

10. Elizabeth K .Cooper, *And Everything Nice, the Story of Sugar and Spice.* Illustrated by Julie Maas (New York: Harcourt, Brace & World, 1966).

11. O. Glenn Blough and Julius Schwartz, *Elementary School Science* (New York: Holt, Rinehart & Winston, 1964).

ment fails because of something neglected in the process of doing the experiment. Sometimes it fails because steps in the tradebook were not accurate. Then other tradebooks need to be consulted for verification or rejection of the steps and/or information. When experiments are repeated, different children should be in the roles of the experimenters.

The experiments should be accompanied by much discussion to make certain that the purpose, techniques, and conclusions are clear, thus strengthening concept formation. The experiment from a tradebook can become the children's own experiment through a free discussion and planning for the experiment. The purpose and the way in which the procedures accomplish the purpose should become clear and acceptable to the children. It is well to have discussion of the experiment at the various stages of experimentation; there should be interaction before the experiment is initiated, during the experiment, and after the experiment has been completed.

The summary is an important phase of an experiment. Concept development must not be overlooked, and summarizing is an attempt to stress the rational process and the learned generalization. It is important that the summary of the experiment not be limited to the process of convergent thinking—equal emphasis must be given to divergent thinking. There is a need for a summary which not only repeats the known but which also encourages the learner to move toward the unknown. Illustrations of the divergent orientation are questions like the following: What are possible applications of what we have learned today? What are some questions it raises in your mind? Suggest other experiments to test the idea. What are some other things that you would like to know about the topic?

Huck and Kuhn have stated:

> The science activity or experiment book should be designed to guide children in making their own discoveries. Open-ended questions, guides to observation, and suggestions for further study are strategies that lead to pupil problem-solving. . . . Writers who can develop ability to observe, relate facts, summarize and generalize are contributing to the child's understanding of science concepts and skill in using methods and tools of science.[12]

Now Try This,[13] by the Schneiders, is an example of a book that guides the child to discover basic principles for himself. The pattern is the same for each experiment:

12. Charlotte S. Huck and Doris Young Kuhn, *Children's Literature in the Elementary School*, 2d ed. (New York: Holt, Rinehart & Winston, 1968), pp. 457-58.
13. Herman and Nina Schneider, *Now Try This*. Illustrated by Bill Ballantine (New York: William R. Scott, 1947).

"Let's Find Out" — (purpose of the experiment)
"Try This" — (procedure)
"You Will Find" — (observation of result)
"Now You Know" — (conclusions) and
"You Found Out" — (principle)

In summary, rich experimentation includes freedom to explore. A steady diet of step-by-step patterns is limited in its potential for freedom to explore. It is restrictive in nature. Scientists must learn both to follow instructions and to invent procedures. There is a need for equal emphasis on the second aspect—the creator. Therefore, in selecting and using experiment tradebooks, teachers must insure that both aspects are emphasized.

Play and Dramatics

Dramatic play for the younger children and the more highly organized dramatics of the older children, as related to the unit, contribute to the meeting of intellectual needs through clarification and assimilation of information. Play and dramatics are of great value also in meeting emotional-social needs in that, through these activities, children relieve tensions and strains, gain status, security, and a feeling of belonging.

Characters and concepts encountered in print become real to children as they identify with the characters or concepts through creative dramatics. Through creative performance, boys and girls step into the shoes of the characters, and they "feel" the characters, the settings, and the scenes. A child may read about a blind man; his teacher may ask him to relate the man's inner feelings. But until he has "been" that blind man himself, the child cannot really do so.

Dewey Chambers wrote:

> Creative drama is a short, structured dramatic play activity, wherein the emphasis is placed on the process, rather than on the product. It should be spontaneous and creative; it should show depth of insight into the characters played and the issues involved; it should be free of formalized theatrics; and it should provide satisfaction, if not real delight, to those who involve themselves with it. It is a natural part of childhood which can easily and successfully be employed by teachers of elementary school students.[14]

Menagh stated:

> The requirements of creative dramatics are few, consisting only of a group of children with a qualified leader and a space in which to

14. Dewey W. Chambers, *Literature for Children: Storytelling and Creative Drama* (Dubuque, Iowa. Wm. C. Brown Company Publishers, 1970), p. 53.

function. There is no need for a script or for the technical aids so frequently associated with theatre production . . . no scenery, lighting, costumes or make-up. The only physical environment required is a space such as almost any classroom can provide with the tables and chairs pushed back. These tables or desks and chairs may, of course, be used from time to time. There is no audience but that possibly provided by the participants themselves.[15]

Once a selection for creative performance has been made, youngsters should discuss character and plot development and play out the characters as they "feel" the roles they take on. The teacher's major concern is with the process and the values for the children involved. The value lies in the process of playing. Dialogue may be added, and although lines may become somewhat finalized, they are usually neither written nor memorized.

The main thrust of pantomime and dramatization found in some tradebooks will tie in with many topics in social studies. *Fried Onions and Marshmallows and Other Plays for Little People*[16] is a collection of short plays which are fun to read aloud or produce just as they are, with or without scenery. Many are based on folktales, and young actors will enjoy portraying already-familiar characters. *The Complete Book of Children's Theater*[17] contains in a single volume rearranged material from eight earlier books by Howard: *Holiday Monologues, Humorous Monologues, Charades and Pantomimes, Puppet and Pantomime Plays,* and others.

There can be dramatization of folktales and fables, of people in books about other lands, and of people in biography. Boys and girls might play the roles of people they are reading about in the past, in history, as well as people in other places or situations.

Creative dramatics is not confined to interpreting a complete story or poem. Creative dramatics may be for the purpose of interpreting a concept. Instead of words that may scarcely move one inch from their sluggish beginning on a printed page, youngsters have a better feel for a concept as they are involved in the many twists and turns of interpreting that concept. And there are times when two books lend themselves to the creative interpretation of the same concept.

15. H. Beresford Menagh, "Creative Dramatics," in *Guiding Children's Language Learning*, ed. Pose Lamb (Dubuque, Iowa: Wm. C. Brown Company Publishers, Second Edition, 1971), p. 83.
16. Sally Melcher Jarvis, *Fried Onions and Marshmallows and Other Plays for Little People*. Illustrated by Franklin Luke (New York: Parents Magazine Press, 1968). Ages 3-8.
17. Vernon Linwood Howard, *The Complete Book of Children's Theater*. Illustrated by Doug Anderson and others (Garden City, N. Y.: Doubleday & Co., 1969). Ages 9 and up.

For example, *I Never Saw Another Butterfly*,[18] is an intermixture of prose and poetry written by children of the Terezin concentration camp. *The Me Nobody Knows*,[19] 1968, is prose and poetry by black children and young people living in a ghetto. The concept of "ghetto" and the voices of the ghetto are found in both books.

The Me Nobody Knows is a collection of the writings of students in ghetto schools in New York City. There are poems, stories, letters, and essays by nearly two hundred children, ranging in age from seven to eighteen. The book is divided into four sections: "How I See Myself," "How I See My Neighborhood," "The World Outside," and "Things I Cannot See or Touch." Most of the writing is concerned with what the children know best—the ghetto, that city within every city. Spelling and grammar are uncorrected because Mr. Joseph believes that "The children should feel free to speak without fear of being evaluated." Of what significance is a misplaced comma if a child is trying to express the reality of his existence? The eternal themes of love, sleep, death, darkness also appear in the book.

In October 1941, the Germans established a concentration camp at Terezin, thirty-seven miles from Prague. The camp was designed as a "model" which could be shown to the International Red Cross, but its function was to be a way station for the transports to Auschwitz and other death camps. By August of 1942, 41,552 Jewish prisoners lived at Terezin. From 106 to 156 people died every day. Among the population were thousands of children. By May 1945, when the Soviet army liberated Terezin, about 15,000 children under fifteen had passed through Terezin. Of these, about 100 survived. *I Never Saw Another Butterfly* is a book of pictures and poems created by some of the children who lived at the camp. The poems, drawings, water colors, and collages, have been gathered from the State Jewish Museum in Prague. Children's education was intensively carried on by the prisoners at Terezin. They taught the fundamentals of drawing. Poetry contests and recitations were held, and instruction in literature was conducted in secret. Civilization, in short, was carried on by the prisoners themselves even as they were caught within a system opposed to all civilizing processes. The book bears witness to this. There are tiny, quick drawings of guards and keepers. There is a little girl carrying her numbered suitcase as she stands at the barbed wire, ready for transport. The endpapers are

18. *I Never Saw Another Butterfly*. Children's drawings and poems from Theresienstadt Concentration Camp 1942-1944 (New York: McGraw-Hill Book Co., 1964).
19. Stephen M. Joseph, ed., *The Me Nobody Knows*. Children's Voices from the Ghetto (New York: Avon Books, 1969).

a lyric pattern made out of the ever-present screen of barbed wire. Here in this combination of word and image, we see reflected, not only the daily misery of these uprooted children, but a degree of courage and optimism that is their triumph.

Poems from the two books should be read. The boys and girls may select the poems they think can be dramatized, as well as the ones they wish to dramatize. Questions should guide the children's understanding of the characters, setting, and scene development. But youngsters' spontaneity should not be drummed out of them. Their freshness should come through. If we trust them, they will come up with interpretation. We are too much accustomed to plays where everything is drummed in and everyone has a place to go. But creative dramatics must be just that—creative dramatics. It must be improvisational. Each time it is done, it will become more real even though interpretations are done by different youngsters. Afterwards, there should be time for discussion. Picard's *One Is One*, Sterling's *Mary Jane*, and Estes' *The Hundred Dresses* are other noteworthy books which lend themselves to creative dramatization.

Creative dramatics—selecting, preplanning, guiding questions, feeling the situation, building the character, discussing plot development, playing, evaluating, replaying, new players, and new interpretations. But in the end, always applying what has been experienced and interpreted toward better working and living together. For that is what social studies and life are all about.

Crafts and Construction

Construction is another way of learning directly since it involves the use of data gained through observation, experimentation, and manipulation. Construction activities contribute to meeting the basic needs of children. It is most natural for young children to put things together, using various kinds of simple materials. For satisfactory results involving construction activities, there must be careful planning.

Tradebooks permit youngsters to research information for construction projects. Having secured the information, they put it to use as they construct and create.

Two books by Peggy Parish would be helpful in units related to early America and to Indians of North America. *Let's Be Early Settlers*[20] contains explicit instructions for making a variety of pioneer objects. Sunbonnets, model log cabins, dioramas of forts and flatboats are a few of the handicraft and construction suggestions given. The simple

20. Peggy Parish, *Let's Be Early Settlers* (New York: Harper & Row, Publishers, 1967). Ages 6 to 10.

textual instructions are supplemented by lively line drawings. *Let's Be Indians*,[21] by the same author, is another book of easy-to-follow instructions for forty-one Indian projects, including things to make, games, and sand painting. Among the projects, all of which utilize readily available materials, are a complete Indian costume, cornhusk mats and dolls, pottery, a bow and arrow, a drum, ceremonial masks, three model Indian villages, pipe cleaner figures, and peanut puppets. The book is illustrated with many drawings and would be useful in connection with creative and dramatic play as well.

Collage and Construction[22] gives sensible advice on materials and techniques. Firm adherence to aesthetic precepts, and a broad spectrum of media make this a better-than-most books on art experience. The media discussed include box pictures, paper collage, wire sculpture, and string pictures.

Fun with Your Fingers: Working with Sticks, Paper, and String[23] contains clear, simple directions for making a variety of useful and decorative objects from inexpensive, easily obtainable materials. Paper folding and cutting; string painting; weaving on a handmade cardboard loom with bamboo sticks, dried cornhusks, weeds, or nylon hosiery strips, as well as yarn; and unweaving are some of the skills described. Originality and creativity are stressed throughout the book, qualities which make the book highly recommendable. Upper elementary grade pupils would be able to read and use the book on many occasions.

Directions for making, dressing, and performing with puppets, plus three suspenseful puppet plays is found in *Hand Puppets,* by Laura Ross. Another informative book is *Be a Puppeteer,* by Worrell.

Making Easy Puppets,[26] by Shari Lewis, gives easy-to-follow directions for making thirty-six simple puppets out of handkerchiefs, paper, fruit, paper bags, balls, gloves, and other easily obtained materials. There are also directions for making or improvising puppet stages, suggestions for keeping a "rainy-day box," and ideas for having fun with the puppets. This book would be helpful in grade three to six with almost any unit of study.

21. Peggy Parish, *Let's Be Indians*. Drawings by Arnold Lobel (New York: Harper & Row, Publishers, 1963). Ages 5 to 10.
22. Harvey Weiss, *Collage and Construction* (New York: William R. Scott, 1970). Ages 9 to 12.
23. Harry Helfman, *Fun with Your Fingers: Working with Sticks, Paper, and String*. Illustrated by Robert Bartram (New York: William Morrow & Co., 1968).
24. Laura Ross, *Hand Puppets: How to Make and Use Them*. Illustrated (New York: Lothrop, Lee & Shepard, 1969). Ages 8 and up.
25. Estelle Ansley Worrell, *Be a Puppeteer: The Lively Puppet Book* (New York: McGraw-Hill Book Co., 1969). Ages 8 and up.
26. Shari Lewis, *Making Easy Puppets*. Illustrated by Larry Lurin (New York: E. P. Dutton & Co., 1967).

Creating Mosaics[27] is an unusual book to which youngsters in the upper elementary grades should have access as they consider various construction possibilities. The book gives suggestions and directions, supplemented by many two-color drawings, for creating mosaics out of a variety of materials including paper, eggshells, seeds, cereals, clay tiles, pebbles, bottles, and dishes. The projects progress from a simple mosaic made of scraps of paper cut from a magazine advertisement to tile mosaics and to mosaic murals constructed by a group. While the instructions are explicit enough to be easy to follow, they allow for experimentation, and they encourage creativeness.

What can you do with sand? Beginning with this ingredient common to all beaches, *The Beachcomber's Book*[28] leads the beachcomber through the making of sand lanterns, pebble mosaics, shell mobiles, into the finer arts of driftwood sculpture and beach glass design. Creative achievement is within the grasp of every child, whether he chooses to assemble a shell collection, build an aquarium, or make a driftwood lamp. The book is sprinkled lightly with palatable facts about shells and seaweed, tides and marine life. The careful, explanatory text should enable even the youngest to combine imagination with the fascinating bounty of the sea and create his own masterpiece. The fine drawings illustrate each project with clarity and humor. This lively, enlightening volume gives a fresh glance at the pleasures and treasures of a sandy beach.

Rags, Rugs, and Wool Pictures[29] is an easy-to-use book describing the techniques of rug hooking—from creating designs to completing them.

Aesthetic Activities

In a sense, this is not a distinctive category, since the materials and techniques of art, with emphasis upon the beautiful, are involved in varying degrees in all the other types of activities. Some activities, however, seem to be primarily aesthetic, and it is these that are included in this grouping.

The art of various countries is vividly portrayed in tradebooks, for example, *The Art of India*,[30] by Shirley Glubok. In her latest explor-

27. James E. Seidelman and Grace Mintonye, *Creating Mosaics.* Illustrated by Harriet Sherman (New York: Crowell, Collier & Macmillan, 1967).
28. Bernice Kohn, *The Beachcombers Book.* Illustrated by Arabell Wheatley (New York: Viking Press, 1970). Ages 6 to 11.
29. Ann Wiseman, *Rags, Rugs and Wool Pictures.* Illustrated with photographs (New York: Charles Scribner's Sons, 1968).
30. Shirley Glubok, *The Art of India* (New York: Macmillan Co., 1969). Ages 12 and up.

ation of exotic cultures, the author uses the magnificent classic art of India as a guide to the three major religions which have played such a dominant part in the development of this ancient civilization. As she comments, knowledge of this art helps us understand how millions of Indians think and live and worship today. *Made in Ancient Egypt*[31] provides a gateway to the wonders of ancient Egyptian art. An unusual book of art is found in *Celebrate the Sun*.[32] All in full color, reproductions of fifty-one extraordinary paintings by children from all over the world capture the joys of festivals and seasonal change. A page of the text explains the significance of the festival shown in the picture on the facing page.

The music, dance, and rhythms of countries, eras, and cultures will also add to understandings and feelings for countries and people.

American Indians Sing[33] is excellent in showing the importance of music in the daily life and in the special ceremonies of the American Indian. The lucid text, amply supplemented by drawings, photographs, transcribed musical selections, and a recording, describes some of the instruments and basic dance steps and explains the purpose and performance of the significant songs, dances, and musical rituals of major Indian tribes throughout the country. The book shows the relatedness of music, daily life and ceremonies making it an excellent source for children and young adults.

Yankee Doodle[34] is a colorful picture book interpretation of this ten-verse song about the Yankee soldiers during the Revolutionary War. Included are simple arrangements for the verses, brief historical notes about the song, and a recipe for hasty pudding.

Singing Soldiers: A History of the Civil War in Song[35] is a book of selections and historical commentary by Paul Glass. Delightful old prints illustrate an impressive collection of songs arranged for piano or guitar accompaniments to the melodic line. The long and informative preface, the notes preceding each selection, and the lyrics of the songs do indeed have historical value, and the bibliography is useful.

31. Christine Price, *Made in Ancient Egypt* (New York: E. P. Dutton & Co., 1969). Ages 10 and up.

32. Betty Nickerson, *Celebrate the Sun* (Philadelphia: J. B. Lippincott Co., 1969). Ages 10 and up.

33. Charles Hofman, *American Indians Sing*. Drawings by Nicholas Amorosi (New York: John Day Co., 1967). Ages 8 to 12.

34. Richard Schackburg, *Yankee Doodle*. Illustrated by Ed Emberley. Notes by Barbara Emberley (Englewood Cliffs, N. J.: Prentice-Hall, 1965). Ages 4 to 8.

35. Paul Glass, *Singing Soldiers: A History of the Civil War in Song*. Musical arrangements by Louis Singer (New York: Grosset & Dunlap, 1969). Ages 11 and up.

If American folk music or the period from the 1870's to the 1880's is a part of any unit of work, *Cowboys and the Songs They Sang*,[36] by Samuel John Sackett, would be an enriching tradebook. Music and words for fourteen popular cowboy songs, together with authentic old photographs of ranch and trail activities and the author's simple nomenclature and descriptive commentary present an entertaining, enlightening picture of cowboy life in the days of the great cattle drives. The songs chosen illustrate major interests and concerns of the cowboy.

London Bridge Is Falling Down[37] is a picture book version of the well-known nursery song. It includes many verses, plus a brief history of the bridge and music for the song. Both familiar and new, the 109 selections in *The Small Singer*,[38] by Roberta McLaughlin and Lucille Wood, are chosen to "help small singers find their singing voices." There are songs about little creatures, nature, special days (Thanksgiving, Halloween, Hanukah, etc.), songs to play to, with suggestions for rhythm instruments and acting, songs for home, songs about pets, wheels and wings, Mexico, and patriotic American songs. Piano arrangements are simple, guitar chords are provided, and the color illustrations of Jacques Rupp romp nicely along in the happy spirit of the book.

John Langstaff's *Hi! Ho! The Rattlin' Bog and Other Folk Songs for Group Singing*[39] presents fifty songs suitable for somewhat older children—sea chanteys, work songs, lullabies, question-and-answer songs, folk hymns, counting songs, riddle songs, jig tunes, historical songs, simple part-songs, dance songs, narrative ballads, ghost songs, laments, calypso songs, and chorus songs. Brief notes explore their origin and meanings, arrangements are fresh and original and easy to play, and basic guitar harmonies are indicated. Black and white drawings by Robin Jacques are reminiscent of old-fashioned steel engravings and give added appeal to a very rich collection.

Folk Songs of China, Japan, Korea[40] was edited by Dietz and Park. This book includes an authentic recording of the songs and gives the pronunciation of words in the original language.

36. Samuel John Sackett, *Cowboys and the Songs They Sang*. Settings by Lionel Nowak. Designed by Walter Einsel (New York: William R. Scott, 1967). Ages 9 to 12.
37. Peter Spier, *London Bridge Is Falling Down*. Illustrated by Peter Spier (Garden City, N. Y.: Doubleday & Co., 1967). Ages 5 to 8.
38. Roberta McLaughlin and Lucille Wood, *The Small Singer* (Glendale, Calif.: Bowmar Publishing Corp., 1969).
39. John Langstaff, *Hi! Ho! The Rattlin' Bog and Other Folk Songs for Group Singing* (New York: Harcourt, Brace & World, 1969).
40. Betty Warner Dietz and Thomas C. Park, eds., *Folk Songs of China, Japan, Korea* (New York: John Day Co., 1964).

In *A Fiesta of Folk Songs from Spain and Latin America*,[41] there are thirty-four folk songs, including singing games and dances, songs for Christmas, and songs about people, animals, and nature—songs which are sung and loved by children of Latin America and Spain. Piano arrangement and guitar chords are given, together with the original Spanish lyrics, their phonetic pronunciation and their English translations. A brief description introduces each song.

A Scottish Songbook[42] is beautifully and hilariously illustrated by Evaline Ness and deserves to be treasured in anyone's collection of books. Each of the sixteen airs is a story and a poem as well as a song, with themes ranging from the droll and pawky (mischievous, cunning, sly) to tender and melancholy ballads. Songs of love and thrift and loneliness, written by King James V of Scotland, Allan Ramsey and Alexander Boswell, eldest son of James, are to be read as well as sung. Simple melodies are provided for voice and piano, along with guitar chords. There is a glossary of Scottish words and meanings.

Savez-Vous Planter les Choux?[43] is a charming collection of twenty-nine French songs dating from the fifteenth to the nineteenth centuries. There are songs from the provinces, songs which began as political lampoons, songs of military origin, songs with many verses telling amusing stories, singing games with steps and gestures, and even one little operetta. Guitar chords are indicated, with simple melodies for voice or piano. Small children who are learning French, as well as adults, will find the book suitable. In *The Sounds of Time*,[44] the parallel development of man and his music from ancient Egypt to the present is depicted with sixty-seven photographs and prints, and two maps aiding the interpretation.

Socially Useful Experiences

No learning can be more valuable for children than that which culminates directly in the actual improvement of living. Children should be helped and encouraged to contribute to public safety, to community health, to civic beauty, to the protection and conservation of resources and materials, and so on. An educated person needs to be more

41. Henrietta Yurchenco, comp., *A Fiesta of Folk Songs from Spain and Latin America*. Illustrated by Jules Maidoff (New York: G. P. Putnam's Sons, 1967). Ages 7 to 12.

42. Sorche Nic Leodhas, *A Scottish Songbook* (New York: Holt, Rinehart & Winston, 1969). Ages 10 and up.

43. Anne Rockwell, *Savez-Vous Planter les Choux?* (New York: World Publishing Co., 1969).

44. Nancy Wise Hess and Stephanie Grauman Wolfe, *The Sounds of Time: Western Man and His Music* (Philadelphia: J. B. Lippincott Co., 1968). Ages 11 and up.

than someone who has mastered a set of facts. He needs to be some-one who is sensitive to other people, who can communicate with other people, and who can feel emotions. Socially significant work can help youngsters become educated in this sense. Socially significant work, sometimes referred to as School and Community Services, would be those kinds of activities whereby youngsters do things for others even though they don't have to do so. Involvement in these services means a reali-zation that it is the common and decent thing to do something for others.

Tradebooks by their very content can lend to discussion of social-ly significant action. They help raise and answer the question: "What can we do to help?" The first example centers on the current problem of noise pollution, and the second is of mental retardation. The topic of communication would be related to the third example.

There are several tradebooks whose topic is "sound." Only a few will be mentioned here.

Sound and Ultrasonics,[45] by Ira Freeman, is one of the first titles in the new Random House Science Library and is a revised edition of *All About Sound and Ultrasonics.* The original book has undergone some rewriting, and new material has been added. It has also been redesigned and newly illustrated with eye-catching photographs and drawings and would be especially useful in grades four to eight. *Sound and Hearing,*[46] by Charles Gramet, is an informative introduction to the science of sound. It explains the nature of sound waves, the func-tions of the human voice, and the production of musical sounds. It de-scribes the structure of the human ear and the various mechanical de-vices for amplifying, recording, and communicating sounds, including the use of satellite relay stations and laser beams. There is also a chapter on ultrasonic sound waves. There are explanatory diagrams and useful supplementary materials for the study of sound and communication.

High Sounds, Low Sounds,[47] suitable for grades one to three, is an enjoyable introduction to the physics of sound. It explains pitch in terms of fast and slow vibrations, and it touches on the physiology of hearing. As with other books in this series, humorous illustrations re-inforce the ideas expressed in a very simple text.

45. Ira Freeman, *Sound and Ultrasonics.* Illustrated by George Resch (New York: Random House, 1969).

46. Charles Gramet, *Sound and Hearing.* Illustrated by Leslie Howard (New York: Abelard-Schuman, 1965).

47. Franklyn M. Branley, *High Sounds, Low Sounds.* Illustrated by Paul Galdone. (*Let's Read and Find Out Science Books*) (New York: Thomas Y. Crowell Co., 1967).

A highly comprehensive book is *The World of Sound*,[48] by Irwin Stambler. The nature of sound, the physiology of the human voice and ear, and the invention and function of various mechanical devices for producing, transmitting, and receiving sounds are among the topics covered in a detailed explanatory text supplemented by diagrams and photographs. The author also discusses present and possible future uses of ultrasonic sound in medicine, agriculture, industry, and in the exploration of sea and space. This is truly a serviceable book on the science of sound.

Your Ears,[49] by Irving and Ruth Adler, would be helpful in grades four to six. The structure and physiology of the ear, the nature of sound, and the types of deafness are explored in this simple, concise account. Although not up to the authors' usual standards, it will be useful with additional material. For ages four to eight, there is *Sound Science*,[50] by Melvin Alexenberg. Included are easy experiments about sound which will inspire the very young.

These tradebooks easily lead to a natural consideration of noise pollution. And noise pollution should be related to socially significant activities for youngsters.

One physicist, Dr. Vern Knudsen, has predicted that if noise continues to increase at the present rate, in thirty years the downtown areas of our largest cities will be as deadly as the ancient noise tortures used by the Chinese to execute condemned prisoners. The greatest incidence of assault upon the ears, not surprisingly, takes place in industry. And even without any additional problems, we are already at the point where untold numbers of men, women, and children are suffering disabilities due to noise. The United States lags behind other nations which long ago recognized noise as an environmental pollutant and adopted national laws to deal with it.

Boys and girls might discuss what they can do to help the growing problem. If one wants to avoid adverse effects of noise pollution, one can:

—turn down the record player
—be more considerate about horn honking

48. Irwin Stambler, *The World of Sound* (New York: W. W. Morton & Co., 1967). Grades 6 and up.
49. Irving and Ruth Adler, *Your Ears*. Illustrated by Peggy Adler Walsh (New York: John Day Co., 1965).
50. Melvin Alexenberg, *Sound Science*. Illustrated by Tomic de Paola (Englewood Cliffs, N. J.: Prentice-Hall, 1968).

—encourage reduction of the volume of jet plane noise by encouraging the changing of flight paths

—plant more trees (Trees and grass absorb noise and diffuse sound waves. When used as barriers, says the U.S. Department of Agriculture, they can reduce noise by as much as 65 percent.)

—start an Anti-Noise Drive

—inform the public through use of posters at shopping centers

—write to Hearing Conservation, Inc., Upper Montclair, New Jersey, for brochures and information on the subject. Plan to condense and share these materials with parents.

—write to congressmen urging codes such as are found in England, France, Germany, and the Scandinavian countries.

The Second Example

Children often know and live near a mentally retarded child without understanding the feelings of this child and without knowing what they can do to help. *Don't Take Teddy*[51] is translated from the Norwegian by Lise Some McKinnon. Teddy is fifteen, a mentally retarded child whose younger brother, Mikkel, is fiercely protective. When, quite by accident, Teddy hurts another child, Mikkel runs away with him, leaving a note for their parents. He is afraid that Teddy will be put into an institution. By the time the two boys reach the summer cottage where Mikkel plans to hide, they are both ill from fatigue and exposure. Mikkel realizes that Teddy is a heavy burden, but he accepts the idea of placement in a special school only when he learns that Teddy will have day care and will return to his family each evening. This is quite a remarkable book because the author teaches a lesson without preaching. In Mikkel's love for his brother, there is a realistic embarrassment but no shame; there is a realistic range of reactions from people he meets, and a realistic acceptance of the limits of the educability of the retarded. The book is a plea for understanding, but the plea is not made directly by the author; by having the story told by Mikkel, the communication is more direct and most touching. Once again, questions and answers related to "What We Can Do to Help" can add to better understanding and better living in schools, in neighborhoods, in communities.

Communication is of concern to elementary youngsters, either as a unit in itself or as a topic within a unit. Tradebooks on this topic can be found at all levels. In a socially significant activity called Care-Ring, youngsters can be involved in a unique telephone service for the lonely—those people who may be laid up with the flu for several weeks,

51. Babbis Fris-Baastad, *Don't Take Teddy* (New York: Charles Scribner's Sons, 1967). Ages 10 and up.

or the elderly shut-ins, the infirm, and the like. Often these people receive no calls, or at best, perhaps one call from a distant relative. Other than that brief communication, their phones may be silent all the time. The involved youngster is a companion who says, "I am someone who cares." The conversation may be a mixture of weather information, TV and radio suggestions, and cheerful chit-chat. Any of this would be a high point in the bleak routines of those persons shut off from others. The calls may lead to or be followed up with birthday cards, pen-pal relationships, and even the introduction of one lonely person to another. Youngsters thus become involved in relevant communication rather than "playing at" communicating.

Tradebooks, in themselves, can be stories of socially significant work. *Welcome Child*,[52] by Pearl Buck, was written because the author believes that all children who have no parents should find parents. If their parents are dead, or if they have been forgotten, then adopted parents must be found for the child. And that is what Pearl Buck does quite often through an adoption agency called Welcome House. The child in the picture book, *Welcome Child*, was a child who came through Welcome House. Pearl Buck wanted to tell the story of one such child—how, at first, the child was afraid but then became accustomed to Americans and living in America. It is a true story about a true little girl. And it is a story of socially significant work.

Tradebooks can point to socially significant work that would be possible in the future lives of boys and girls. For example, there are numerous tradebooks on the topic of conversation, a topic studied in elementary schools, and one of national concern. Congress has created a Youth Conservation Corps. The minimum age for corpsmen is sixteen years. The corps, patterned after the Civilian Conservation Corps of the 1930's, gives about 3000 young people the opportunity to reseed forest land, help fight forest fires, maintain trails and campsites, and undertake other conservation work. This is a three-year pilot program and involves girls as well as boys. Socially significant work thus becomes related to current events and to the future lives of boys and girls.

In summary, it seems clear, from this chapter, that tradebooks are the lifeline of a unit of instruction—from its conception to its culmination.

Tradebooks are also the lifeline of textbook learnings. They enhance textbook teaching by providing for a wide-range of reading levels which cannot be provided for with a single social studies text. And tradebooks offer up-to-date information—information which is often outdated in the textbooks found in many classrooms.

52. Pearl Buck, *Welcome Child* (New York: John Day Co., 1964).

chapter 8

science education program

The American Association for the Advancement of Science sponsored a major study in 1961.[1] The study was designed to review the status of elementary school science and to formulate a plan for improvements. In addition to advocating the merit of major focus on problems of elementary school science education, this report stressed that "cognitive processes" be given special emphasis at the elementary school level.

Thus the report highlighted an issue in science education which began to assume considerable importance: the relative stress to be given to "content" goals and "process" goals. In one approach, the content of a discipline as it is viewed by academicians is the primary source of innovation. Here the basic principles underlying the field are identified by scientists in an attempt to underscore the conceptual unity of a subject and to counteract what some have perceived as the triviality of the content taught previously. An underlying assumption of this viewpoint is that there is a relatively small number of pervasive ideas within any discipline. If one can identify these ideas, one has a basis for developing a stable program for students below the college level.

In the "process" approach, as reported by Gagné,[2] the most basic attribute of science, particularly for young learners, is the method by which scientists engage in their investigations. Scientists observe. They measure. They classify. They infer. "Process skills" are generalizable over many science fields. Major efforts should be given to the identification of these skills and their inclusion in school programs. This view-

1. Thomas S. Hall, et al., "Science Teaching in Elementary and Junior High Schools," *Science* 133 (1961):2019-24.
2. Robert M. Gagné, "Elementary Science: A New Scheme of Instruction," *Science* 151 (1966):49-53.

point is close to the one accepted during the 1930's; however, in its more recent form, scientists have played a more prominent role in identification and description of the methods used in scientific investigation. During the 1930's, few scientists displayed interest in curriculum construction below the college level.

Most schools seem to be developing or accepting programs that stress both facets of science—the conceptual aspects and the methodological aspects; it is probably impossible as well as undesirable to separate the two completely. Noteworthy tradebooks, wisely used, can contribute to the realization of both the "content" and the "process" goals.

If the content goal of science education is to be met, certain standards for tradebooks become immediately significant. There must be accuracy and authenticity of information, with supporting facts for generalizations. Illustrations should clarify the content which should be recent and current. Interrelationships of facts and principles should be shown so that the reader does not become lost in a welter of bits and pieces of information. Because of the limited amount of material in some tradebooks, the teacher must insure comprehensive information either by providing additional sources or by at times himself providing facts for youngsters. In using the tradebooks, critical reading must be in evidence. For example, facts should be distinguished from theory. Tradebooks can also be used to extend information found in textbooks and very often are more up-to-date than the "aged" publication dates of some textbooks found in classrooms.

Tradebooks may, in fact, meet all designated criteria, but the manner in which they are used may undermine the author's efforts in writing an effective and noteworthy tradebook. Activities, observations, experiences are suggested in science books but often are misused for concept development because of overstructured methodology and a steady diet of specific questioning from teacher to pupil.

The pursuit of excellence calls for the education of the individual as a creator. Bruner says:

> For whatever the art, the science, the literature, the history and the geography of a culture, each man must be his own artist, his own scientist, his own historian, his own navigator.[3]

A major contribution of science methodology to the development of the "scientist" in the learner is its emphasis on the process of discovery. In terms of learning, to discover is not mainly to find some-

3. Jerome S. Bruner, *The Process of Education* (Cambridge, Mass.: Harvard University Press, 1960), p. 116.

thing new, but to find something for oneself. Inquiry precedes discovery. The teacher who rushes to answer questions rather than to guide children to inquire may be short-cutting the process of discovery.

Let us examine the following illustration reported by Wood where youngsters were manipulating bar magnets as suggested in a science tradebook:

> A pupil manipulates the bar magnet and exclaims: "Why are there so many paper clips at the two ends?" The teacher responds: "This is because the magnets are strongest at the ends. We call these end poles. What do we call them, children?"[4]

The example demonstrates how a teacher takes the shortest possible route between the question and the answer. The pupils may have gained information, but they did not experience the process of inquiry or discovery on their own. The teacher, though well-meaning, might have responded: "This is an interesting observation. How can we find the answer?" The principle involved suggests an extension of the process of inquiry which takes place between the question and the concluding answer. Methodology should not be overstructured and too constrictive in nature. There should be freedom for exploration as the child moves step by step toward a predetermined goal.

A steady diet of specific step-by-step questioning by the teacher may be harmful to developing a child's creativity. The following record illustrates how some teachers lead children through systematic and specific questioning following a tradebook suggestion that youngsters experiment with seeds . . . explore and observe various seeds.

> Teacher: What do you see?
> Child: Little brown seeds.
> Teacher: How are they different?
> Child: They are different colors and shapes.
> Teacher: (Distributes some lima beans that have been soaked in water.) Are the wet beans larger?
> Child: They are larger than the dry ones.
> Teacher: How is the skin?
> Child: Softer.
> Teacher: Try to peel it off.
> Child: It is easy to do it.
> Teacher: What is inside?
> Child: A baby plant.

4. Anne Helen Wood, "Science Teaching," mimeographed (New York: Brooklyn College, 1964).

There is no attempt here to underestimate the strength of this approach to observation. It is experiential in nature and leads to meaningful concepts about seeds. It generally arouses the enthusiasm of primary school children. However, despite this positive contribution, the example illustrates the spoon-feeding of step-by-step structuring. In reply to a question, the child's function is limited to one answer. "Are the wet beans larger than the dry beans? Are they softer? Where is the baby plant?"

In developing this lesson, it is possible to replace the scores of minute questions with one major task: "Observe the seeds (apple, dry, and wet lima beans), touch them, feel them, look at them, see what you can find out about them. Then later, tell me what you found out and give me any questions you came up with." Under this arrangement, the child has to work on his own or in small groups for a certain period, putting things together and creating his own sense of order. The teacher's function is to guide the discussion and further observation on the basis of the oral reports given later. Despite the fact that, in both approaches, children may come out with similar information, in terms of processes of thinking they travel through different routes. In the first instance, as each question is answered, the child waits for the second question before moving on. In the second instance, the teacher guides the discovery in a different manner whereby the learner is free to go ahead on his own.

If step-by-step questioning on the part of the teacher is the usual procedure, then we limit the potential for youngsters to raise questions. It is unfortunate when, with very few exceptions, all questions in lessons are raised by the teacher. Both Getzels[5] and Torrance[6] assess the ability to raise questions and identify problems as one of the indices of creative thinking. The ability to raise questions is as important as the ability to find the answer.

A major approach in developing the ability of children to identify problems is to provide for open-ended situations. Often, materials are distributed to the group and their manipulation encouraged. Such manipulation leads the pupils to make discoveries of scientific relations. For instance, to discover the principles of buoyancy, the following materials are suggested in one tradebook:

5. Jacob Getzels, *Creativity and Intelligence* (New York: John Wiley & Sons, 1962).
6. Paul E. Torrance, *Education and the Creative Potential* (Minneapolis: University of Minnesota Press, 1963).

A dish of water for each group of four children. Things which float, like wood. . . . Things which sink, like marbles, a penny. . . . Things which sink and float, like plastic sponges.

Small groups could then be instructed to see what they can find out and to record the questions which they want to raise for general class discussion. After a period of free experimentation, the teacher calls on the children to join in discussion of their findings and questions. This approach can be used effectively with many of the tradebook suggestions for observation and experience.

Using tradebooks in science education needs to be more than reading and telling about. Tradebooks must be integrated with firsthand experiences. Youngsters need to observe, classify, measure, record, experiment, and generalize. Wise use of the available bounty of science tradebooks requires a reduction in the controlling functions often exercised by teachers. The stereotyped question-and-answer blocks children's use of higher mental processes. Only as pupils experience, pupils question, pupils discover—only then will clear, lucid science concepts be developed.

chapter 9

mathematics education

In the conventional classroom, there may be one graded mathematics textbook series through which the children proceed, page by page, lesson by lesson, with problem exercises for reinforcement. The teacher presents the idea, does some sample problems, and the children then do other similar problems. Only one book may be used, but each child has a copy.

Many teachers, however, recognize the wide range in ability and achievement that they have in any group of children of the same chronological age. To remedy the problem, they may group children for instruction and use books written for different levels of achievement and ability. Such a procedure calls for a variety of tradebooks to clarify, extend, and reinforce concept learnings.

Tradebooks should hold a prominent place in the instructional program. Their many vivid illustrations make them a strong resource for learning experiences. Tradebooks often explore the many twists and turns of a concept to a greater degree than can be done in page limitations of textbooks. Tradebooks are vehicles for adjusting the mathematics curriculum to the differences in abilities and interests which are obvious to all sensitive and observant teachers.

In the experience-centered approach to learning, tradebooks are necessary. However, they are not the only basis for learning mathematics. Dealing only at the abstract level is not conducive to understanding. There must be appropriate use of materials for youngsters to manipulate. Manipulative materials and follow-up activities are necessary to clarify and extend concepts introduced in tradebooks.

"Discovery" is one of the most important aspects of mathematics education, and providing appropriate manipulative materials is essential for this type of learning. Firsthand experience with objects is a basis for Piaget's concrete operational level of thought. Children should

be allowed to perform the necessary physical manipulations or concrete operations that are necessary for real learning of mathematical
concepts. The youngster solves problems for himself as a basis for learning rather than having ideas "explained." The child is placed in a situation in which he discovers for himself. He explores, observes, sorts,
organizes, classifies, measures, compares, questions, and discovers.

At all grade levels, children need to use manipulative materials to reinforce the mathematical ideas found in tradebooks. Such materials
might include wooden blocks, dried peas or beans, match boxes, felt
cutouts of different shapes and colors, plasticene, milk straws, sand,
pipe cleaners, popsicle sticks, tongue-depressor sticks, counting frames
such as a coat hanger with wooden beads on it; measuring tools; and
for place-value concepts, an abacus and pocket charts. Seashells, golf
tees, marbles, beads, buttons, bottle caps, clothespins, play money,
old clocks, watches, egg timers, scales, cash registers, cups and spoons
of all sizes will aid the youngsters in concept learning.

Containers are needed for most of these materials. Large sheets
of polyethylene are needed as a floor or table cover when working with
sand, as also are tools for transferring sand. And containers that hold
the same amount but that are different in shape should be provided.

More expensive but also useful are various commercially prepared
materials, such as logic blocks, trundle wheels, stop watches, mathematical balances, Cuisenaire rods, Diene's Multibase Arithmetic Blocks,
Multimat; and geometric models, including a sphere, cube, rectangu-
lar solid, cylinder, and triangular prisms.

To explore geometric or spatial relationships, the pegboard is a
very useful device. Rubber bands can be fitted on the pegs or nails
to represent the various basic shapes, and such ideas as perimeter and
area relationships can be explored.

Measurement is an important part of science and mathematics when
the youngster is ready for it. There are many materials needed for experiences in measurement. These include balance scales, weights, rul-
ers, yardsticks, tape measures, meters, trundle wheels, various sized
plastic containers, and ribbons of different colors and lengths. Several tradebooks deal with measurement. Lines of different lengths are
shown in the illustrations. Youngsters are asked which is longer, shorter, and so on. But children must do more than "point to" and respond
to the tradebook queries. For example, in studying length, the children
may compare ribbons of different colors and lengths. At first, the lengths
and colors should match those found in the illustrations of the tradebooks or should answer questions found in the tradebooks. Youngsters
may be first asked which is longer, the red or the black? Which is short-

er? And finally, to "order" the ribbons by finding the shortest, the next longer, and so forth. They should order from shortest to longest and also from longest to shortest. Later, lengths which go beyond those found in the tradebook should be explored.

One important reminder: When using instructional materials, one should not assume that an entire classroom of children must necessarily be doing the same thing at the same time. There are often occasions, of course, when it is appropriate to introduce a concept to the entire class. But there are many occasions when this is not appropriate, given differences in learning pace and style.

Even within the constraints of a self-contained classroom with one adult and thirty children, an imaginative teacher may devise numerous ways to utilize these manipulative materials so that small groups, or individuals within the class, may simultaneously be working on different activities. For example, many games lend themselves to being played independently by children with tape-recorded instructions and with immediate feedback through individual answer sheets. Colored slides in an automatic carousel-type projector, operated by the child, may be used to present and to answer some of the problems. Another possibility is the use of pupil tutors. With older elementary pupils, an additional technique is to provide written instructions to guide independent or small-group learning. And, of course, there are often times when the teacher may work with one group while other pupils are engaged in more abstract paper-and-pencil reinforcement activities.

There are times when ideas or activities will be useful with several tradebooks. Examples follow. More than one tradebook deals with geometric shapes. A "feel box" is a covered cardboard box with holes cut in the sides large enough for a hand to reach through. Geometric shapes are placed in the box, and the children are asked to remove the shape the teacher describes. Each child gets a point for removing the correct shape. A variation of the game can be played by having children select any shape from the feel box. Points may be earned by correctly identifying the selected shape before they remove it from the box and see it.

A "number-numeral" game is another game which can be used with several tradebooks. The teacher constructs cards which are divided into nine squares (three squares horizontally and three squares vertically). A numeral from 0 to 9 is placed in each square, using a different order on each card. Each pupil should be given a card along with nine counters. To play the game, each child who has the numeral on his card corresponding to the number depicted in an illustration or on a page of a tradebook covers it with a counter. The child whose card is covered first wins. In a large group, several children may win simultaneously. Several variations are possible by making the winner the first child to cover the vertical center row, or to complete some other pattern.

Several tradebooks are concerned with teaching direction, visual perception, area, properties of geometry, and rational numbers. Geoboards will help youngsters make determinations in building those concepts. On a 9″ x 9″ square board, twenty-five nails are placed in five horizontal and five vertical rows at 1½″ intervals. Rubber bands of various colors are used to reproduce figures and lines. The boards may be used according to the following suggestions: (1) reproducing horizontal, vertical, and diagonal lines; (2) reproducing geometric shapes; (3) adding fractional parts to find combined area; (4) discovering propreties of angles (we use two segments to form an angle, placed so they have one point in common—vertex); (5) finding coordinates (mark boards with letters and numerals).

"One-to-one matching" game will involve the pupils in another manner. The children place one stick or counter on their desks for each object found in specific illustrations or pages of a tradebook.

Having made suggestions which apply to the topics of several tradebooks in the math bibliography, ideas for use with specific tradebooks are now given.

Robert Allen's *Numbers*[2] is replete with concept development possibilities. The first third of the book enumerates familiar items, from one kitten and two eggs to ten cookies. The second part indicates that numbers do not necessarily occur in sequence, and that "how many" does not necessarily mean "how much." For example, if there are six marbles in a short row, and six marbles in a long row, the number of marbles is the same. The third part of the book teaches simple addition—one puppy and one puppy equals two puppies, and so on. Appropriate questioning and manipulation of materials are necessary for the wise use of illustrations. Illustrations in and of themselves do not guarantee understanding. Let us use the pictures of the six marbles as an example. Matching of objects in one set with objects in another set is a prelude to counting. In comparing two sets—are they the same (in number), or is one larger? Which one? How much larger? This is in sharp contrast to the way children have often learned to count by simply memorizing a sequence of sounds—"one, two, three, etc."— or by simply repeating the sequence of sounds in the tradebook. The

2. Robert Allen, *Numbers*. Photographs by Mottke Weissman (Bronx, N. Y.: Platt & Munk, 1968).

futility of such a process is seen by asking a child to tell you how many objects (marbles) you hold in your hand. If he has just learned to memorize a sequence of sounds, he is unable to match the number names with objects in your hand. He has not established the idea of one-to-one correspondence that is basic to counting. Number is an idea, or abstraction, and not an object in the physical world, but it does need a physical framework in which to develop for children. Dogs, cars, houses are objects in our physical world, but a "two" is not. Concrete objects (felt cutouts, small toys, marbles) must accompany the use of tradebooks dealing with numbers.

In *Brian Wildsmith's 1, 2, 3's*,[3] an outstanding illustrator utilizes basic abstract forms—the circle, the triangle, and the rectangle—in combination with brilliant color to create a stimulating and beautiful counting book. The eye-catching pictures, all of which are kaleidoscopic in design, begin with a single circle representing the number one, and progress to recognizable objects, such as an owl which is composed of ten geometric shapes. An additional four pictures test the child's understanding of the pictorial presentation and the one-page textual explanation. The book is an exciting visual and informative experience. Youngsters could find how many models of triangles, squares, rectangles, and circles there are in the classroom (such as the chalkboard as a rectangle). If at all possible, they should make a graph showing the number relation between these different shapes.

Size, Distance, Weight: A First Look at Measuring[4] will facilitate concept development in measurement. The book is remarkably clear and explains common units of measurement in terms of objects and experiences familiar to young children. The economical text objectifies units of length and distance, weight, volume, time, and temperature, as well as several special-purpose measurements. A brief description of the metric system shows its simplicity in contrast to nonmetric systems. The many drawings are most valuable. Activities will add dimensions to the several concepts explored in this book. Four are given as examples here. The teacher will think of many more.

The flannel board and various cutouts of objects can demonstrate which objects have the same, or different, heights, lengths, or overall sizes. Objects (each kind together) are placed on the board, and the children may be asked the following:

3. Brian Wildsmith, *Brian Wildsmith's 1, 2, 3's* (New York: Franklin Watts, 1965). Ages 3 to 7.
4. Solveig Paulson Russell, *Size, Distance, Weight: A First Look at Measuring*. Illustrated by Margot Tomes (New York: Henry Z. Waldcock, 1968). Ages 5 to 9.

"Find two pieces of yarn that are the same length."
"Find two rectangles that are not the same height."
"Find the largest piece of yarn."
"Find the smallest rectangle."
"Find the largest triangle."

A variation of the above might be to give the pieces of yarn and various cutouts to youngsters, have them work in small groups, and come up with observations of their own ("These two pieces are the same length." "This is the largest piece of yarn." "This is the smallest rectangle." etc.).

A second experience related to the book would be to collect sand, water, and containers of various sizes and shapes. Children should experiment by filling different containers with sand or water. They should keep records by drawing pictures of containers which hold the most, the same amount, or least. Or they might write a description or make a chart based on their observations.

Thirdly, milk containers can be used to discover relationships of cups, half-pints, pints, quarts, half-gallons, and gallons. Pupils pour quantities from one container to another to show equivalent standard units of measure. A record of the results can be kept by having children place cutouts of the containers on the bulletin board, or even the actual cardboard containers tacked in place.

A fourth experience would be to use a measuring tape to record a classmate's shadow at hourly intervals between 11 A.M. and 2 P.M. Lengths of string are cut for the shadow lengths and are fastened side by side on the wall or on a large sheet of cardboard, so that pupils can compare how they changed.

Children should be encouraged to compare objects—to determine the relationships that exist between their characteristics or properties and the properties of other objects. Mathematics is a study of relationships. Is one object heavier, lighter, darker, smoother, rougher, bigger, smaller, taller, shorter, thicker, thinner, the same shape? Younger children will study such relationships; later they will measure to make more precise determinations. It is necessary that the children themselves make these determinations as in a laboratory setting for a real idea of number and geometry to develop. It is necessary that these activities accompany the use of tradebooks in classroom instruction.

An understanding of the use of sets involving arithmetical problems is developed in progressive steps, from the simple identification of sets of familiar objects to sets composed of symbols in Sets[5] by Irving

---

5.   Irving and Ruth Adler, *Sets* (New York: John Day Co., 1967). Grades 3 to 6.

and Ruth Adler. Clear, simple explanations of each unit are supplemented by examples and, in some cases, charts and diagrams are followed by practice exercises. The book is of practical value as a supplement to mathematical studies in grades 3 to 6. *Sets and Numbers for the Very Young*,[6] published in 1969 by the same authors, explains the "new math" to the very young. The book is especially useful for children in the four to six age range.

There can be assignments with tradebooks, but the assignments are not in terms of pages or problems. Instead, there is extracting of ideas. The child is provided a situation from which he should discover for himself or "disengage" the mathematical structure involved. For example, with the latter tradebooks, there may be the following assignment on a card:

1. Get the bag of logic blocks and empty them in the place where you work.
2. Put them in sets so that they are like the sets in the book.
3. Put them in sets so that they are alike in some way. Write down how each set is alike.
4. Can you group them so that they are alike in another way? Write how they are alike now.
5. Are there still other ways that they can be grouped so that they are alike? If so, write the other ways they are alike.

String, Straightedge and Shadow[7] is the story of geometry. This book is a history of man's thinking about forms in nature, their use in construction, and finally, the abstract rules of geometry. The illustrations by Bell will be enjoyed by intermediate grade youngsters. Pegboards and pegs may be used as well as nailboards, or commercial Geoboards with colored rubber bands to explore properties of geometric shapes and line designs. Children can reproduce geometric shapes, create designs, and find solutions to problems such as "How many triangles can I make from one square unit?"

Although there is an overabundance of cartoon-like drawings and instructional diagrams in *Shapes*,[8] this book will prove valuable for concept development. Using the process of discovery method of presentation which encourages the child to draw appropriate conclusions from demonstrated or observed data, the author supplements her ex-

6. Irving and Ruth Adler, *Sets and Numbers for the Very Young* (New York: John Day Co., 1969). Ages 4 to 6.
7. Julia Diggins, *String, Straightedge and Shadow* (New York: Viking Press, 1965). Grades 5 and 6.
8. Jeanne Bendick, *Shapes* (New York: Franklin Watts, 1968). Grades 2-4.

planations of shapes, lines, planes, and three-dimensional figures and symmetry with stimulating questions and problems. Because of the wide scope and complexity of some of the concepts discussed, the book will also be of benefit in some classrooms when used in connection with science units. Manipulative activities should follow the introduction of this book. Using string, wire, yarn, or straws, children could construct squares, rectangles, and triangles. Flannel shapes would serve as the basis for a second activity. Pupils close their eyes while the position of a geometric shape on a flannel board is changed. A shape may be moved by changing its position or by placing it in a different spot on the board. Finding shapes whose positions have been moved provides good observation experiences. A game of very simple and inexpensive materials would add another dimension to the development of these concepts. A large spinner and sets of cards containing geometric shapes in colors can be made. The spinner would include the same shapes which are found on the sets of cards. There should be a set of cards for each child. As the spinner indicates a shape of a certain color, children show their cards matching the shape.

Much of our knowledge comes, not from without, but from within by the forces of our own logic. Since much of our knowledge comes from within, this means it does not come directly from the teacher. A basic responsibility of the teacher will be to provide a physical environment and a questioning technique that provoke the logical processes within the mind of the child, processes which are necessary for concept development.

One of the great values of the kinds of well-written tradebooks, manipulative materials, and accompanying activities which have been described briefly here is that they promote pupil involvement in learning and help the child to explore and discover basic mathematics concepts for himself.

The attempt here has been to show the different types of books which may facilitate the development of mathematical concepts. Different kinds of activities have been suggested, some of which would relate to the general themes of several books, and some of which would be usable with specific books only. The teacher will continually add to her repertoire of activities as she explores the many tradebooks listed in the annotated bibliography on mathematics.

part

three

the

aesthetics

chapter 10

music

There is a wide range of tradebooks for music and art education. Numerous books give information about instruments of the orchestra and about the composition of music. *The First Book of Music,*[1] by Norman, and *All about the Symphony and What It Plays,*[2] by Commins, are examples of books from series that give interesting information. Kettlekamp's book, *Horns,*[3] is the fourth in his series about instruments. These small books would be especially useful as children make decisions about the instruments they want to learn to play. Also, the author shows how to make simple instruments. Chappel has designed beautiful books based on the theme and music of *The Sleeping Beauty* and *The Nutcracker.*[4] Bulla has written good background stories for the Wagner opera, *The Ring and the Fire: Stories from the Nibelung Operas Retold.*[5]

Most children begin to read about music after learning to like it— but the reverse is possible, and a well-illustrated, well-written book such as Joseph Wechsberg's *The Pantheon Story of Music for Young People*[6] might do just that. Wechsberg, a professional violinist before he became an author, is a graceful, lucid stylist, and he outlines the history of music fluently. The major facts are here, brightened by an occasional laconic

1. Gertrude Norman, *The First Book of Music.* Illustrated by Richard Gackenbach (New York: Franklin Watts, 1964).
2. Dorothy B. Commins, *All about the Symphony and What It Plays.* Illustrated by Warren Chappel (New York: Random House, 1967).
3. Larry Kettlekamp, *Horns* (New York: William Morrow & Co., 1964). Grades 4 to 6.
4. Warren Chappel, *The Sleeping Beauty* (New York: Alfred A. Knopf, 1967). Also *The Nutcracker* (New York: Alfred A. Knopf, 1968).
5. Clyde R. Bulla, *The Ring and the Fire: Stories from the Nibelung Operas Retold.* Illustrated by Clare and John Ross (New York: Thomas Y. Crowell Co., 1967).
6. Joseph Wechsberg, *The Pantheon Story of Music for Young People* (New York: Pantheon Books, 1968).

comment ("extremely gifted men who had the bad luck to live in the wrong time") and apt references to our time.

The stress is, naturally, on the classical and romantic eras, partly because those eras produced the music most familiar to the ordinary music lover, and partly because Wechsberg is Viennese, with a deep affection for the Austrian-German repertory. But other periods (Greek, Byzantine to contemporary) get some attention. The pictures are varied; the necessary portraits of composers alternate with paintings, operatic scenes, and drawings.

A complementary volume is *The Wonderful World of Music*[7] just reissued in a revised edition. This is not a chronological report, but rather, a treatment of music's aspects, "Sound and Rhythm," "Songs and Singers," and so forth. It may be of more interest to the young reader than straight history. As a leading contemporary composer, Britten brings a different illuminating viewpoint to the subject, and the book touches on the music of other cultures.

In *Tales from the Ballet*,[8] the stories of twenty ballets—"Petrouchka," "Ondine," "The Firebird" among them—are told step by step as they ritually unfold on stage, along with the thoughts and the imaginary dialogue of the characters. Length of the narratives varies greatly according to the complexity of the plots. But in all of them, storyteller Louis Untermeyer is a master of brevity, clarity, and sensitivity. The emphasis in selection is on the classic repertoire; the ballet of most recent vintage, "Fancy Free," was first produced twenty-four years ago. The tales are complemented by a deftly abbreviated history of ballet and a set of notes about composers, choreographers, designers, themes, librettists, and productions of the individual works. *Tales from the Ballet* will not only answer the child's inevitable "What's happening up there on the stage?" but will also serve as an appealing and unusual storybook as well. With a strain of fond humor, illustrators Alice and Martin Provensen have unerringly captured the spirit and style of musical selections that are ages and cultures apart. Ethereal grace, brilliant Oriental splendor, rustic simplicity, primitive starkness, verve and delicacy are unified by a patina of pastel wash. The result is reminiscent of a rich, gently faded tapestry.

Every Child's Book of Nursery Songs,[9] a collection of ninety-one nursery rhymes (some familiar, some new), and melodies and songs

7. Benjamin Britten and Imogen Holst, *The Wonderful World of Music* (Garden City, N. Y.: Doubleday & Co., 1968). Ages 12 to 16.
8. Louis Untermeyer, *Tales from the Ballet*. Illustrated by Alice and Martin Provensen (Racine, Wisc.: Western Publishing Co., Golden Press, 1968). Ages 6 to 9.
9. Donald Mitchell, *Every Child's Book of Nursery Songs* (New York: Crown Publishers, 1969).

for both family and school, is a remarkable value. Simple and lilting piano accompaniments make it easy for the amateur pianist, and suggestions are included for the use of rhythm instruments and the speaking voice. Decorative pen and ink drawings with water color, by Allan Howard, are in the manner of the famous Staffordshire dogs and cats.

Earl Bichel's *How Many Strawberries Grow in the Sea?*[10] offers twenty-six of the lesser known Mother Goose rhymes which seem especially suited to the humor of little ones who belong to the television generation. "Betty Botter's Batter," "Cakes and Custard," "When I Was a Bachelor," and others are as good for laughing as for singing. Piano arrangements are within reach of the most amateur pianist, and color illustrations by George Suyeoka keep pace well with the jaunty spirit of the collection.

Biographies of musicians, composers, and conductors can play an important part in the music curriculum. Ewen's biographies, *Leonard Bernstein*,[11] *The Story of George Gershwin*,[12] and *The Story of Arturo Toscanini*[13] have a livelier style than do the Wheeler and Buecher biographies, *Ludwig Beethoven and the Chiming Tower Bells*,[14] *Mozart, The Wonder Boy*,[15] and others. Older children will enjoy *Famous Negro Music Makers* by Hughes.[16]

10. Earl Bichel, *How Many Strawberries Grow in the Sea?* (Chicago: Follett Publishing Co., 1969).

11. David Ewen, *Leonard Bernstein* (Philadelphia: Chilton Book Co., 1960).

12. David Ewen, *The Story of George Gershwin* (New York: Holt, Rinehart & Winston, 1963).

13. David Ewen, *The Story of Arturo Toscanini* (New York: Holt, Rinehart & Winston, 1960).

14. Opal Wheeler, *Ludwig Beethoven and the Chiming Tower Bells*. Illustrated by Mary Greenwalt (New York: E. P. Dutton & Co., 1962).

15. Opal Wheeler and Sybil Deucher, *Mozart, the Wonder Boy*. Illustrated by Mary Greenwalt (New York: E. P. Dutton & Co., 1961).

16. Langston Hughes, *Famous Negro Music Makers* (New York: Dodd, Mead & Co., 1955).

chapter 11

art

Tradebooks can be informational resources as they offer guidance for art experiences. *Pastels Are Great*[1] teaches techniques in an art medium, beginning with the way to hold the brush. Showing examples of correct and incorrect strokes; the author explains the varieties of strokes and the effects gained by using each. The reader is urged to experiment; both text and illustrations make the project appear enticing and gay. *Creative Rubbings*[2] introduces a different type of art experience. Starting with the art of making rubbings or recording a pattern in relief on a flat surface, the author and her husband devised a method for creating original designs from which to make rubbings. There are easy-to-follow suggestions for making the original designs and pictures which were made by children, ages seven to ten.

A Picture Is A Picture: A Look At Modern Painting[3] is a perfectly splendid book by art critic W. G. Rogers. He pays his young readers the compliment of addressing them as he would their elders. His discussion is easy to read because the style is clear and convincing. Influential artists and the essentials of major movements are briefly but carefully described. It is a simple authoritative work on the subject. Cartoons and caricatures as art forms unfold in *Mightier Than The Sword*.[4] Fascinating glimpses of artists who have used this medium are presented. The author describes the work of the artists in relation to their times and the influence each had on the contemporary scene.

1. John Hawkinson, *Pastels Are Great* (Chicago: Albert Whitman & Co., 1968). Ages 8 to 10.
2. Laye Andrew, *Creative Rubbings* (New York: Watson-Guptill Publications, 1968). All ages.
3. W. G. Rogers, *A Picture Is A Picture* (New York: Harcourt, Brace & World, 1969). All ages.
4. W. G. Rogers, *Mightier Than The Sword* (New York: Harcourt, Brace & World, 1969). All ages.

Tradebooks can be a motivating or an integrating force in art experiencing. As youngsters view illustrations in tradebooks, they may study and compare different illustrators and media. After reading trade-books, youngsters could draw their own illustrations, their own inter-pretations of the story. The use of specific art techniques may result from stories. For example, descriptive words or passages found in books can be applied to collages and "feeling" pictures in which various tex-tured materials cut in interesting shapes are pasted upon a paper sur-face. Or, as boys and girls consider various books, they could create:

1. A Rogues Gallery, with "Wanted" posters for villains and other undesirable characters met in literature.
2. A World Map of Storybook Characters, where small figures are pinned to the map in the appropriate locations.
3. A "Favorite Characters Corner," which would be a "portrait gallery" for special story characters.

Increasingly, the influence of children's literature is being seen in the theater and on the stage as children's books are translated into other art forms.

It is almost 70 years since Beatrix Potter's creatures first delighted the children of the world. The tiny volumes, 169 million of which have been sold in the U.S. alone since World War II have now been translated with extraordinary fidelity by England's Royal Ballet into a film called "The Tales of Beatrix Potter." The costumes follow Miss Potter's un-mistakable paintings, and the ballets have the same uncluttered spirit as her stories. Potter lovers who are almost literally without number will feast on this fare which is faithful to the original. In another treat, the National Ballet has offered one of its most beautiful and successful ballets in "Cinderella."

Joseph's *The Me Nobody Knows* has become a musical based on an anthology of the writings of children from the slums of New York city. And the cinematography fare for youngsters includes Dahl's *Charlie And The Chocolate Factory*,[6] Juster's *The·Phanthom Tollbooth*,[7] Travers' *Mary Poppins*,[8] and Lamorisse's *The Red Balloon*.[9]

These emergings in the theater, in musicals, and cinematography will allow youngsters the opportunity to broaden their horizons of the humanities and the arts. Happily so. For, the anthropologist, Hoevel, has observed that man could probably survive without the arts, but to do so, he would have to return to an ape level of existence.

5. Stephen Joseph, Editor, *The Me Nobody Knows* (New York: Avon Books, 1969). All ages.
6. Ronald Dahl, *Charlie And The Chocolate Factory* (New York: Knopf, 1964).
7. Norton Juster, *The Phantom Tollbooth* (New York: Random House, 1961).
8. Pamela L. Travers, *Mary Poppins* (New York: Harcourt, Brace, World, 1934).
9. Albert Lamorisse, *The Red Balloon* (New York: Doubleday, 1956).

Laura Graves

chapter 12

literature: and the last shall be first

Because another book in this series deals with the discipline of literature,[1] it is not the responsibility of this writer to deal in detail with that topic. However, it would be remiss not to set forth, though briefly, a philosophy and viewpoint.

Although the title of this book concerns itself with literature in the curriculum, the philosophy of this writer is not to place the utilitarian value of children's books over and/or against its aesthetic value. Literature has a respected, purposeful place of its own in the curriculum. Children's books should not be viewed for instructional purposes alone. They should be viewed as aesthetic experiences also—equally so, rightfully so, purposefully so.

Children's books are a way of teaching facts, principles, and values. They leave in the child's mind a residue of information about people, times, places, processes, and heroes. Books support interest in studying frontier America and all other topics. However, *just as important is the using of books primarily for aesthetic experiences.* These are the times when concern and enthusiasm would be first and foremost for the literary merit of the story at hand. These are the times when pleasure and enjoyment are significant.

The elementary curriculum incorporates a rightful place for literature in and of itself. And the elementary teacher lays plans so that literature is allowed to sieze the heart as well as the mind.

Teachers introduce children to the pleasures of the company of books. For this introduction, teachers play a dual role—only one of which is inside the classroom. The other role is outside the classroom as the teacher helps parents introduce youngsters to the delicacies of printed words. It all begins at home.

1. Bernice E. Cullinan, *Literature for Children: Its Discipline and Content* (Dubuque, Iowa: Wm. C. Brown Company Publishers, 1971).

Parents need more help than merely having lists of books. Parents will need and want advice regarding the using of picture books. Adults should choose a simple book for the very young child. A small youngster is happy to sit on someone's lap and listen to a voice reading almost anything; but if the reading can add to his vocabulary because the pictures and the sounds are identifiable, so much the better. Nursery rhymes may not enthrall the adult, but the child enjoys the rhyme and rhythm. Children love to pore over a book that has been read to them often and to "read" it themselves. If there is a minimum of print, it is that much easier for them to remember and that much more encouraging as a first reading experience.

Parents should know that while visually sophisticated books are often stunning and appealing to adults, clear colors and simple composition are better choices for the very young. Household objects, vehicles, animals, children engaged in familiar pursuits are preferable to busy pages, abstractions, pop art, or grotesque illustrations, no matter how intriguing the adult finds them.

The adult can stimulate the child's interest in books by referring to them and quoting from them. Children delight in making connections between their own experiences and those of fictional friends. Adults should sing the nursery rhymes and play with sounds. The child will be quick to imitate. Stories should be told as well as read. Children should be exposed to storytellers—through recordings such as those made available by Weston Woods, through the neighborhood librarian, and through all other local storytellers. Storytelling enhances a predilection for print, and storytellers, like rare books, are often found in rare places. For example, one of the most exciting storytellers with whom the writer is familiar is a policeman by vocation but an unmatched storyteller by avocation.

The child of three or four is ready for humor and action. He can appreciate a funny story that is realistic, or the comedy in nonsense and exaggeration. He is ready to get ready to read and, therefore, should be encouraged. There should be talk about letter sounds, and nonsense rhymes should be invented with him. If he asks questions about letters and words, the questions should be answered but there should not be insistence on his learning them.

For the young, there are available excellent alphabet, counting, color, concept, and picture books. And for the rare child who does not like fantasy, there should be poetry which can be read to him. When he is almost ready for school, Milne, Potter, and the *Just So Stories* should be read aloud. But, by all means, he should also be given the wonderful books now being published for beginning readers.

He will soon be reading them himself, and parent and teacher—in partnership—will have contributed to a deep pleasure the child will have all his life.

When the child enters school, the teacher takes on an additional role for spiriting a love of books. This is his classroom role. He organizes literature within a humanities framework, a pattern fortunately growing in acceptance. This pattern integrates not only the areas of English but also cuts across subject-matter division and correlates literature with other expressions of man's creativity, for example, with art, music, and drama.

The teaching of literature is part of a planned program for which the main object is enjoyment of literature and continued interest in reading through developing a sensitivity to literary elements as well as to content. The program recognizes characteristics of children, and individual differences. The teacher and the pupils know that the literature being read is the main goal of instruction and not a peripheral objective.

In providing books, the teacher looks respectfully at our rich literary heritage and broadly and expectantly at our own times, A teacher is sensitive to timing a book's significance insofar as it leads to other matters a child may come to know through that book. And the teacher knows when a book is an experience worthy and desirable in itself. In providing a time for books, he is concerned with literature as literature and with the pupil as man. The teacher strives to bring them together so as to ignite a spark that may make the child a better person.

The planned literature program is a daily reality. Reading to the class is the rule and not the exception. This is a very special and uninterrupted time. There is a DO NOT DISTURB sign on the classroom door. Youngsters' favorites are read to them. And they are introduced to the new. There is the literature for sheer delectable enjoyment, and there is the literature for peace—whether that peace comes through laughter or through tears.

For this very special time, there is a very special spot in the room. An adult rocker, a child's rocker, an upholstered chair, pillows, rugs, lamps, and dividers are in evidence. The pillows and rug might be visual representations of some favorite book. For example, one teacher made a *Make Way for Ducklings* pillow. The ducks could be snapped on and off the pillow and placed in different locations so that sometimes the ducks were "in a straight line" and other times they were not. The rug was a vivid image of *Millions of Cats*. Another teacher enticed a local dealer to "give up" a comfortable nine-by-twelve-feet rug for the special center in the classroom. Wall hangings, mobiles, felt and flannel stories would be found here too.

People other than the teacher should be involved in the reading and storytelling. Youngsters, the principal, the librarian, and senior citizens have contributions to make. There should be recordings by storytellers and children's literature authors for listening to again and again. And there will be days when, during this special time, everyone, including the teacher, would be reading to himself—each in his own private world.

And nowhere is it written that intermediate grade youngsters should be deprived of this fare! But, unfortunately, in many intermediate classrooms, a time for literature, like the dodo and the great auk, can no longer be found.

There will be occasions when boys and girls should discuss and talk over the stories, analyzing the writing and considering the meaning of the selection. There will be occasions when this should not be so. There will be times when only a tiny part of a child's response to the books will ever burst into words. A far larger part will be going on in his mind and heart. Those are the times when teachers must not pry out responses. Then, the teacher will be more than satisfied to know that the responses are there and that they may be ready to flower into behavior patterns of a love for hearing and reading literature in the lifetime ahead.

Life is not easy. It is full of needs. Literature has the power to meet these needs.

> Fantasy. Humor. Reality. Magic.
> Fiction and non. Heroes and not.
> Consolation. Solutions to problems. Courage.
> Understanding one's self. And understanding others.
> Accepting one's self. Accepting others.
> Laughter and joy. Integrity and dignity.
> Aloneness. Togetherness.
> Giving and taking.
> Faith. Charity. Hope. And love.

The spark for each of these will be found in the curl of a good book.

part

four

appendices

appendix 1

criteria for informational books[1]

Accuracy and Authenticity
1. What are the qualifications of the author?
2. Are facts accurate?
3. Is the book realistic?
4. Are facts and theories clearly distinguished?
5. Do text and illustrations avoid stereotypes?
6. Is the book up-to-date?
7. Are significant details omitted?
8. Are there supporting facts for generalizations?
9. Are differing viewpoints presented?
10. In geography books, is diversity revealed?
11. In science books, is anthropomorphism omitted?
12. Are phenomena given teleological explanations?

Content
1. Is this a general survey book or one of specific interest?
2. Is the coverage of the book adequate for its purpose?
3. Is the book within the comprehension and interest range of the age for which intended?
4. Do experiment books lead to understanding of science?
5. Are experiments feasible and safe?
6. Does the book show interrelationships of facts and principles?
7. Do science books indicate related social problems?
8. Is the book fresh and original?
9. Does the book help the reader understand the methods of science and social science?

Style
1. Is information given directly or in story form?
2. Is the text interesting and appropriate for the age level intended?
3. Do vivid language and appropriate metaphor create interest and understanding?

1. Charlotte S. Huck and Doris Young Kuhn, *Childrens' Literature in the Elementary School*, 2d ed. (New York: Holt, Rinehart & Winston, 1968), pp. 474-75.

4. Does the style create the feeling of reader involvement?
5. Is the language pattern clear and simple, or heavy and pedantic?
6. Is there an appropriate amount of detail?
7. Does the book encourage curiosity and further study?

Format and Illustration

1. Do illustrations clarify and extend the text?
2. Do different types of media maintain clarity of concepts?
3. Are illustrations explained by captions or labels?
4. Are size relationships made clear?
5. Do size of type and use of space contribute to clarity?
6. Are endpapers used effectively?

Organization

1. Are subheadings used effectively?
2. Do the table of contents and the index help the reader locate information quickly?
3. Does the bibliography indicate sources used by the author, and sources for further reading by children?
4. Do appendixes extend information?

appendix 2

evaluation suggestions

Teacher Self-Evaluation Suggestions
1. Do I have a planned literature program as part of an integrated language arts curriculum?
2. Does my classroom reflect a well-planned, thoughtfully organized body of literature experiences?
3. Do I focus on literature as literature as well as use tradebooks to enhance and enrich studies in other curriculum areas?
4. Is "pleasure" present in my literature program?
5. Is there a balanced program between instruction and the encouragement of individual free reading?
6. Is time for independent reading scheduled and provided?
7. Is time available regularly?
8. Do I guide youngsters into the delights of reading for enjoyment as well as for information?
9. Do I read aloud to the youngsters as a way of introducing them to the best in literature?
10. Does the reading aloud occur in intermediate grades as well as in primary grades?
11. Do I go beyond literature stories in the readers?
12. Are enough tradebooks sufficiently accessible to youngsters in my classroom?
13. Do those tradebooks reflect the diversity of interest, tastes, and abilities present in my classroom?
14. Are my feelings for books reflected in the behaviors I exhibit toward and about books?
15. Am I enthusiastic for and about literature?
16. Do I give literature a respected place in the school program?
17. How many new tradebooks have I read this year?

Pupil Evaluation Suggestions
1. Does he read?
2. Does his attitude reflect a desire to read?
3. Is he "catching" an appreciation for good books?
4. Does he read widely?
5. Does he choose to read for enjoyment?

6. Does he read for personal purposes as well?
7. How much does he read?
8. What does he read?
9. How does he interpret his reading achievement? Is it limited to skill development, or does progress in reading include appreciational and recreational reading?
10. When he evaluates his success in reading, does he include personal reading and appreciation as part of achievement?
11. Does he apply what he reads to his life?

appendix 3

taxonomy of literary understandings and skills[1]

Understands Types of Literature
- Differentiates fiction from nonfiction
- Differentiates prose from poetry
- Recognizes folktale
  Identifies traditional beginnings and endings
  Can locate repetition of phrases and episodes
  Realizes characters are usually stereotypes symbolizing extremes—
      good and evil, pretty and ugly, wise and foolish, timid and brave
  Recognizes that folktales communicate values: loyalty, faithfulness,
      courage
- Recognizes fable
  Identifies talking animals as representative of human characters
  Recognizes that a fable states a moral
- Recognizes myth
  Recognizes that characters are supernatural beings interacting with
      each other or with men
  Recognizes that myths were early man's explanations for natural phe-
      nomena or human behavior
  Recognizes that plight of mankind is expressed in myths
- Identifies realistic fiction
  Compares characters and events with his knowledge to determine
      if story could happen
  Looks for evidence of modern life (housing, transportation)
- Identifies historical fiction
  Finds date if mentioned in text
  Establishes period of history through associating way of life, people,
      or events
- Identifies fantasy
  Recognizes the ways in which an author creates fantasy
      Gives animals the power of speech and thought
      Gives inanimate objects the power of speech and thought

1. Charlotte S. Huck and Doris Young Kuhn, *Children's Literature in the Elementary School*, 2d ed. (New York: Holt, Rinehart & Winston, 1968), p. 688.

Endows human beings with magical power or powers
Manipulates time patterns
Changes sizes of humans
Creates new worlds

Understands Components of Fiction
- Recognizes structure of plot
    Summarizes sequence of events
    Identifies conflict or problems
        Conflict of one character with another
        Conflict between man and his environment
        Conflict of values
        Conflict within the individual
    Looks for the interrelatedness of characters and events
    Identifies contrivance in structure
- Recognizes climax of story
    Identifies details and events that build toward climax
    Identifies methods author uses to build suspense
        Finds examples of foreshadowing
        Notices when conflict is first introduced
        Recognizes author's use of "cliff-hangers"
    Recognizes subplot or parallel plot
    Recognizes flashback as a literary device
    Distinguishes episodic and unified plots
    Recognizes details of denouement
- Recognizes character delineation and development
    Can describe important traits of main characters
    Seeks character clues in illustrations
    Recognizes techniques author uses to reveal character
        Describing character in his surroundings
        Showing him in action
        Listening to him talk
        Revealing his thoughts and reactions to people and events
        Showing what others say and think about him
        Telling how others act toward him
    Seeks causes of behavior of characters
    Looks for consistency in characterization
        Consistency of age, period of history, setting
        Internal consistency of character, language, behavior
    Looks for many facets of character other than a stock figure
    Recognizes what changes occur in the character
    Looks for causes of change in character development
- Recognizes theme of story
    Infers meaning beyond the literal account of story
    Looks for clues to meaning in title
- Recognizes setting—both time and place
    Looks for clues in text and pictures that reveal place settings
        Descriptions of places, landmarks, activities, or people
    Looks for clues in text and pictures that reveal time settings
        Period of history
        Season of the year

Identifies influence of setting on characters and events
Recognizes significance of changes in setting
- Describes author's style or use of words
    Distinguishes between straightforward and figurative use of words
    Identifies consistency of an individual's style in writing and illustrating
    Recognizes function of repetition
    Observes balance of narration and dialogue
    Notices descriptive language, figurative language, and allusions
        Identifies metaphor, simile, and personification
        Recognizes meaning of symbols
        Notices play on words or puns
    Recognizes variety of sentence patterns
    Recognizes authentic speech patterns of character
    Recognizes language patterns that relate mood
- Recognizes point of view
    Distinguishes third person narrator (author is telling the story), first
        person narrator (usually main character telling the story), and
        omniscient narrator (author telling story and thoughts of all char-
        acters, adding analytical comment)
    Recognizes influence of point of view on interpretation of story

Understands Components of Poetry
- Interprets meaning
    Looks for key words, images, symbols for meaning
    Recognizes multiple meanings and ambiguity
    Recognizes point of view
    Recognizes theme
- Looks for imagery in the poem
    Sensory appeal
    Simile
    Metaphor
    Allusion
    Symbol
    Personification
- Can describe diction (poet's choice of words)
    Direct, straightforward
    Conversational
    Ornate or simple
- Recognizes sound effects of poetry
    Recognizes words that make the rhyme
    Identifies rhyme scheme
    Looks for words and phrases that create special effects
        Alliteration
        Assonance
        Onomatopoeia
- Identifies various forms of poetry
    Recognizes story element in narrative form
    Recognizes rhythmical and descriptive form of a lyric
    Recognizes nonsense content and line pattern of limerick
    Recognizes stanza form of sonnet
    Recognizes form and content of free verse

Evaluates Literature
- Understands authors right to achieve purpose
    Recognizes different criteria apply to different types of literature
    Recognizes that details are selected to contribute to effect
    Recognizes that form contributes to effect
    Recognizes that theme, plot, characterization, and style all contribute
        to a unified whole
- Evaluates setting
    Considers effectiveness of setting
        Descriptions appeal to five senses
        Influence of setting on plot and characters clearly shown
    Considers authenticity of setting
        True to facts of history and spirit of the times
        Reflects accurate geographical locale
        True to cultural and social attitudes
- Evaluates plot
    Recognizes significance of plot
    Recognizes fresh, unusual plot
    Identifies trite or overworked plot
    Recognizes well-constructed plot
        Evaluates plausibility of plot
        All events contribute to total purpose of story
        Events are significant for forward movement of the plot
        Events occur logically and naturally as a result of action and
            characters
        Suspense is maintained believably
        Logical and believable events build up to climax
    Economy of incident follows climax
    Structure and pacing of plot appropriate for content
- Evaluates characterization
    Recognizes convincing characterization
        Reveals true emotions
        Shows both strengths and weaknesses
        Language and knowledge consistent with background, environ-
            ment, and age
        Main character described fully
    Evaluates character change
        Characters changed by life events
        Author shows reason for change
        Change consistent with personality of character
    Evaluates worthiness of characters themselves
- Evaluates style of writing
    Recognizes appropriateness of style for purpose, character, total effect
    Recognizes quality of description and sensory impressions
    Recognizes originality in use of language
        Interesting, fresh metaphor
        Colloquial language used appropriately
    Evaluates use of symbol
        Symbol made clear in context
        Symbol appropriate to character, setting, plot

- Evaluates point of view
      Recognizes effectiveness of point of view used
      Decides if choice of point of view was a good one
- Evaluates theme
      Considers effectiveness of presentation
            Easily identified in prose or poetry
            Logically developed from plot
            Does not overpower story
      Considers worthiness of theme
            Universal application to life
            Real significance for human behavior

Applies Knowledge of Literary Criticism
- Uses criteria appropriate for type of literature
      Emphasizes criteria of authenticity of setting to evaluate historical
            fiction
      Evaluates techniques used to create believable fantasy
            Grounds fantasy in reality
            Gradual introduction to the fantastic
            Detailed descriptions of settings and characters
            Characters in story express belief in their situation
      Emphasizes image and sound to evaluate poetry
- Asks appropriate questions to analyze writing technique
- Sees relationships among literary selections
      Recognizes similarity in themes, plots, settings, characters, style
- Recognizes similarities and differences in works of one author or illustrator
- Asks appropriate questions for understanding larger meanings
- Recognizes that literature gives insight into human thought and action
- Applies insights gained through literature to his own life
- Continues to seek new understandings

appendix 4

the John Newbery awards

1922 THE STORY OF MANKIND, by Hendrik Van Loon. New York: Boni Liverwright.

✓ 1923 THE VOYAGES OF DOCTOR DOOLITTLE, by Hugh Lofting. Philadelphia: Stokes (J. B. Lippincott Co.).

1924 THE DARK FRIGATE, by Charles Boardman Hawes. Boston: Atlantic Monthly Press, Little, Brown & Co.

1925 TALES FROM SILVER LANDS, by Charles J. Finger. Illustrated by Paul Honore. Garden City, N. Y.: Doubleday & Co.

1926 SHEN OF THE SEA, by Arthur Bowie Chrisman. Illustrated by Else Hasselriis. New York: E. P. Dutton & Co.

1927 SMOKY, THE COWHORSE, by Will James. New York: Charles Scribner's Sons.

1928 GAY NECK, by Dhan Gopal Mukerji. Illustrated by Boris Artzybasheff. New York: E. P. Dutton & Co.

1929 TRUMPETER OF KRAKOW, by Eric P. Kelly. Illustrated by Angela Pruszynska. New York: Macmillan & Co.

1930 HITTY, HER FIRST HUNDRED YEARS, by Rachel Field. Illustrated by Dorothy P. Lathrop. New York: Macmillan & Co.

1931 THE CAT WHO WENT TO HEAVEN, by Elizabeth Coatsworth. Illustrated by Lynd Ward. New York: Macmillan & Co.

1932 WATERLESS MOUNTAIN, by Laura Adams Armer. Illustrated by Sydney Armer and the author. New York: Longman Green (David McKay Co.).

1933 YOUNG FU OF THE UPPER YANGTZE, by Elizabeth Foreman Lewis. Illustrated by Kurt Wiese. New York: Winston (Holt, Rinehart & Winston).

1934 INVINCIBLE LOUISA, by Cornelia Meigs. Boston: Little, Brown & Co.

1935 DOBRY, by Monica Shannon. Illustrated by Atanas Katchamakoff. New York: Viking Press.

✓ 1936 CADDIE WOODLAWN, by Carol Ryrie Brink. Illustrated by Kate Seredy. New York: Macmillan & Co.

1937 ROLLER SKATES, by Ruth Sawyer. Illustrated by Valenti Angelo. New York: Viking Press.

1938 THE WHITE STAG, by Kate Seredy. New York: Viking Press.

1939 THIMBLE SUMMER, by Elizabeth Enright. New York: Farrar & Rinehart (Holt, Rinehart & Winston).

1940 DANIEL BOONE, by James H. Daugherty. New York: Viking Press.

1941 CALL IT COURAGE, by Armstrong Sperry. New York: Macmillan & Co.

1942 THE MATCHLOCK GUN, by Walter D. Edmonds. Illustrated by Paul Lantz. New York: Dodd, Mead & Co.

1943 ADAM OF THE ROAD, by Elizabeth Janet Gray. Illustrated by Robert Lawson. New York: Viking Press.

1944 JOHNNY TREMAIN, by Esther Forbes. Illustrated by Lynd Ward. Boston: Houghton Mifflin & Co.

1945 RABBIT HILL, by Robert Lawson. New York: Viking Press.

1946 STRAWBERRY GIRL, by Lois Lenski. Philadelphia: J. B. Lippincott Co.

1947 MISS HICKORY, by Carolyn Sherwin Bailey. Illustrated by Ruth Gannett. New York: Viking Press.

1948 THE TWENTY-ONE BALLOONS, by William Pene du Bois. New York: Viking Press.

1949 KING OF THE WIND, by Marguerite Henry. Illustrated by Wesley Dennis. Skokie, Ill.: Randy McNally & Co.

1950 THE DOOR IN THE WALL, by Marguerite de Angeli. Garden City, N. Y.: Doubleday & Co.

1951 AMOS FORTUNE, FREE MAN, by Elizabeth Yates. Illustrated by Nora Unwin. New York: Aladdin (E. P. Dutton & Co.).

1952 GINGER PYE, by Eleanor Estes. New York: Harcourt, Brace & World.

1953 SECRET OF THE ANDES, by Ann Nolan Clark. Illustrated by Jean Charlot. New York: Viking Press.

1954 . . . AND NOW, MIGUEL, by Joseph Krumgold. Illustrated by Jean Charlot. New York: Thomas Y. Crowell Co.

1955 THE WHEEL ON THE SCHOOL, by Meindert DeJong. Illustrated by Maurice Sendak. New York: Harper (Harper & Row, Publishers).

1956 CARRY ON, MR. BOWDITCH, by Jean Lee Latham. Boston: Houghton Mifflin Co.

1957 MIRACLES ON MAPLE HILL, by Virginia Sorenson. Illustrated by Beth and Joe Krush. New York: Harcourt, Brace & World.

1958 RIFLES FOR WATIE, by Harold Keith. Illustrated by Peter Burchard. New York: Thomas Y. Crowell Co.

1959 THE WITCH OF BLACKBIRD POND, by Elizabeth George Speare. Boston: Houghton Mifflin Co.

1960 ONION JOHN, by Joseph Krumgold. Illustrated by Symeon Shimin. New York: Thomas Y. Crowell Co.

1961 ISLAND OF THE BLUE DOLPHINS, by Scott O'Dell. Boston: Houghton Mifflin Co.

1962 THE BRONZE BOW, by Elizabeth George Speare. Boston: Houghton Mifflin Co.

1963 A WRINKLE IN TIME, by Madeleine L'Engle. New York: Farrar (Farrar, Straus & Giroux).

1964 IT'S LIKE THIS, CAT, by Emile Neville. Illustrated by Emil Weiss. New York: Harper & Row, Publishers.

1965   SHADOW OF A BULL, by Maia Wojciechowska. Illustrated by Alvin
       Smith. New York: Atheneum Publishers.

1966   I, JUAN DE PAREJA, by Elizabeth Borten de Trevino. New York:
       Farrar, Straus & Giroux.

1967   UP A ROAD SLOWLY, by Irene Hunt. Chicago: Follett Publishing
       Co.

1968   FROM THE MIXED-UP FILES OF MRS. BASIL E. FRANKWEI-
       LER, by E. L. Konigsburg. New York: Atheneum Publishers.

1969   THE HIGH KING, by Lloyd Alexander. New York: Holt, Rinehart
       & Winston.

1970   SOUNDER, by William H. Armstrong. New York: Harper & Row,
       Publishers.

1971   THE SUMMER OF THE SWANS, by Betsy Byars. New York: The
       Viking Press.

1972   MRS. FRISBY AND THE RATS OF NIMH, by Robert C. O'Brien.
       New York: Atheneum.

appendix 5

the Caldecott awards

1938 ANIMALS OF THE BIBLE, A PICTURE BOOK. Text selected from the King James Bible by Helen Dean Fish. Illustrated by Dorothy O. Lathrop. Philadelphia: Stokes (J. B. Lippincott Co.).

1939 MEI LEI, by Thomas Handforth. Garden City, N. Y.: Doubleday & Co.

1940 ABRAHAM LINCOLN, by Ingri and Edgar Parin d'Aulaire. Garden City, N. Y.: Doubleday & Co.

1941 THEY WERE STRONG AND GOOD, by Robert Lawson. New York: Viking Press.

1942 MAKE WAY FOR DUCKLINGS, by Robert McCloskey. New York: Viking Press.

1943 THE LITTLE HOUSE, by Virginia Lee Burton. Boston: Houghton Mifflin Co.

1944 MANY MOONS, by James Thurber. Illustrated by Louis Slobodkin. New York: Harcourt, Brace & World.

1945 PRAYER FOR A CHILD, by Rachel Field. Pictures by Elizabeth Orton Jones. New York: Macmillan Co.

1946 THE ROOSTER CROWS, by Maud and Miska Petersham. New York: Macmillan Co.

1947 THE LITTLE ISLAND, by Golden MacDonald. Illustrated by Leonard Weisgard, Garden City, N. Y.: Doubleday & Co.

1948 WHITE SNOW, BRIGHT SNOW, by Alvin Tresselt. Illustrated by Roger Duvoisin. New York: Lothrop, Lee & Shepard Co.

1949 THE BIG SNOW, by Berta and Elmer Hader. New York: Macmillan Co.

1950 SONG OF THE SWALLOWS, by Leo Politi. New York: Charles Scribner's Sons.

1951 THE EGG TREE, by Katherine Milhous. New York: Charles Scribner's Sons.

1952 FINDERS KEEPERS, by Will (William Lipkind). Illustrated by Nicolas (Mordvinoff). New York: Harcourt, Brace & World.

1953 THE BIGGEST BEAR, by Lynd Ward. Boston: Houghton Mifflin Co.

1954 MADELINE'S RESCUE, by Ludwig Bemelmans. New York: Viking Press.

1955   CINDERELLA, by Charles Perrault. Illustrated by Marcia Brown. New York: Charles Scribner's Sons.

1956   FROG WENT A-COURTIN', by John Langstaff. Illustrated by Feodor Rojankovsky. New York: Harcourt, Brace & World.

1957   A TREE IS NICE, by Janice May Udry. Illustrated by Marc Simont. New York: Harper & Row, Publishers.

1958   TIME OF WONDER, by Robert McCloskey. New York: Viking Press.

1959   CHANTICLEER AND THE FOX, edited and illustrated by Barbara Cooney. New York: Thomas Y. Crowell Co.

1960   NINE DAYS TO CHRISTMAS, by Marie Hall Ets and Aurora Labastida. New York: Viking Press.

1961   BABOUSHKA AND THE THREE KINGS, by Ruth Robbins. Illustrated by Nicolas Sidjakov. Berkeley: Parnassus Press.

1962   ONCE A MOUSE, by Marcia Brown. New York: Charles Scribner's Sons.

1963   THE SNOWY DAY, by Ezra Jack Keats. New York: Viking Press.

1964   WHERE THE WILD THINGS ARE, by Maurice Sendak. New York: Harper & Row, Publishers.

1965   MAY I BRING A FRIEND?, by Beatrice Schenk de Regniers. Illustrated by Beni Montresor. New York: Atheneum Publishers.

1966   ALWAYS ROOM FOR ONE MORE, by Sorche Nic Leodhas. Illustrated by Nonny Hogrogian. New York: Holt, Rinehart & Winston.

1967   SAM, BANGS AND MOONSHINE, by Evaline Ness. New York: Holt, Rinehart & Winston.

1968   DRUMMER HOFF, by Barbara Emberley. Illustrated by Ed Emberley. Englewood Cliffs, N. J.: Prentice-Hall.

1969   THE FOOL OF THE WORLD AND THE FLYING SHIP, by Arthur Ransome. Illustrated by Uri Shulevitz. New York: Farrar, Straus & Giroux.

1970   SYLVESTER AND THE MAGIC PEBBLE, by William Steig. New York: Simon & Schuster.

1971   A STORY—A STORY, by Gail E. Haley. New York: Atheneum.

1972   ONE FINE DAY, by Nonny Hogrogian. New York: The Macmillan Company.

appendix 6

a selected tradebook bibliography*

*When grade levels are not indicated, "all grades" are intended.

ORAL LANGUAGE

ETS, MARIE HALL. *Talking Without Words.* New York: The Viking Press, Inc., 1968. Preschool - Kindergarten.

HUMPHREY, HENRY. *What Is It For?* New York: Simon & Schuster, Inc., 1969. Grades 1-5.

HUPP, LORETTA BURKE. *?Que Sera?* Traditional Spanish Riddles. New York: The John Day Company, Inc., 1969. Grades 3 and up.

LANE, SELMA. *My Book about Me.* New York: Random House, Inc., 1969. All ages.

SCHICK, ELEANOR. *Making Friends.* New York: The Macmillan Company, 1969. Preschool - Grade 1.

SHOWERS, PAUL. *How You Talk.* Illustrated by Robert Galster. New York: Thomas Y. Crowell Company, 1967. Grades 2-4.

TASHJIAN, VIRGINIA. *Juba This and Juba That.* Illustrated by Victoria de Larrea. Boston: Little, Brown and Company, 1969. Grades 1-3.

POETRY

BARNSTONE, ALIKI. *The Real Tin Flower; Poems about the World at Nine.* Drawings by Paul Giovanapoulas. New York: The Macmillan Company, 1968. Grades 5-9.

BOUDIN, JEAN, AND MORRISON, LILLIAN. *Miranda's Music.* Drawings by Helen Webber. New York: Thomas Y. Crowell Company, 1968. Grades 6-8.

KAUFMANN, WILLIAM I. *UNICEF Book of Children's Poems.* Harrisburg, Pa.: Stackpole Books, 1970.

LEAR, EDWARD. *The Scroobious Pip.* Completed by Ogden Nash. Illustrated by Nancy Burkert. New York: Harper & Row, Publishers, 1968. Grades K-4.

MERRIAM, EVE. *Independent Voices.* Drawings by Arvis Stewart. New York: Atheneum Publishers, 1968. Grades 5-7.

SMITH, JOHN, comp. *My Kind of Verse.* Decorations by Uri Shulevitz. New York: The Macmillan Company, 1968. Grades 3-9.

SNYDER, ZILPHA KEATLEY. *Today is Saturday.* Photographs by John Arms. New York: Atheneum Publishers, 1969. Grades 4-6.

STARBIRD, KAY. *The Pheasant on Route Seven.* Illustrated by Victoria de Larrea. Philadelphia: J. B. Lippincott Co., 1968. Grades 5-8.

YEO, WILMA. *Neverbody's Recipes.* Illustrated by Aliki. Philadelphia: J. B. Lippincott Co., 1968. Grades 1-3.

WORDS AND LANGUAGE

ADAMS, J. DONALD. *The Magic and Mystery of Words.* New York: Holt, Rinehart & Winston, Inc., 1963.

APPLEGATE, MAUREE. *The First Book of Language.* New York: Franklin Watts, Inc., 1962.

ASIMOV, ISAAC. *Words in Genesis.* Boston: Houghton Mifflin Company, 1962.

———. *Words from History.* Decorations by William Barss. Boston: Houghton Mifflin Company, 1968.

———. *Words on the Map.* Boston: Houghton Mifflin Company, 1962.

———. *Words from the Myths.* Boston: Houghton Mifflin Company, 1961.

BARTLETT, SUSAN. *Books: A Book to Begin On.* Illustrated by Ellen Raskin. New York: Holt, Rinehart & Winston, Inc., 1968.

BELTING, NATALIE. *The Sun Is a Golden Earring.* New York: Holt, Rinehart & Winston, Inc., 1962.

BENDICK, JEANNE. *A Fresh Look at Night.* New York: Franklin Watts, Inc., 1963.

BREWER, E. C. *A Dictionary of Phrase and Fable.* 8th edition. New York: Harper & Row, Publishers, 1964.

BRICKER, HARRY, AND BECKWITH, YVONNE. *Words to Know.* Illustrated by Dan Siculan. Garden City, N.Y.: Doubleday & Company, Inc., 1969.

BROWN, MARCIA. *Peter Piper's Alphabet* (Subtitle: Peter Piper's Practical Principles of Plain and Perfect Pronunciations). New York: Charles Scribner's Sons, 1959.

CAVANAH, FRANCES, in collaboration with ELIZABETH L. CRANDALL. *Freedom Encyclopedia: American Liberties in the Making.* Illustrated by Lorence F. Bjerklund. Chicago: Rand McNally & Co., 1968.

CHAPMAN, BRUCE. *Why Do We Say Such Things?* New York: Miles-Emmett, 1947.

CLIFFORD, ETH. *A Bear before Breakfast.* New York: G. P. Putnam's Sons, 1962. Grades K-3.

DAVER, ASHEK. *Talking Words: A Unique Alphabet Book.* Indianapolis: The Bobbs-Merrill Co., Inc., 1969.

EPSTEIN, SAMUEL, AND EPSTEIN, BERYL. *First Book of Words.* Illustrated by Laszlo Roth. New York: Franklin Watts, Inc., 1954. Grades 3-5.

———. *The First Book of Words, Their Family History.* Illustrated by Laszlo Roth. New York: Franklin Watts, Inc., 1954.

ERNST, MARGARET S. *In a Word.* New York: Alfred A. Knopf, Inc., 1939.

EVANS, BERGEN. *Comfortable Words.* New York: Random House, Inc., 1962.

FERGUSON, CHARLES. *The Abecedarian Book.* Boston: Little, Brown & Co., 1964.

FOLSOM, FRANKLIN. *The Language Book.* New York: Grosset & Dunlap, Inc., 1963.

FRASCONI, ANTONIO. *See Again, Say Again.* Illustrated by Antonio Frasconi. New York: Harcourt, Brace & World, Inc., 1964.

———. *See and Say.* Illustrated by Antonio Frasconi. New York: Harcourt, Brace & World, Inc., 1955.

FRIEND, M. NEWTON. *Words: Tricks and Traditions.* New York: Charles Scribner's Sons, 1957.

FUNK, CHARLES. *Heavens to Betsy! and Other Curious Sayings.* New York: Harper & Row, Publishers, 1955.

———. *A Hog on Ice and Other Curious Sayings.* New York: Harper & Row, Publishers, 1948.

FUNK, CHARLES, AND FUNK, CHARLES, JR. *Horsefeathers and Other Curious Words.* New York: Harper & Row, Publishers, 1958.

FUNK, WILFRED. *Word Origins and Their Romantic Stories.* New York: Grosset & Dunlap, Inc., 1950.

GOUDEY, ALICE E. *Houses from the Sea.* Illustrated by Adrienne Adams. New York: Charles Scribner's Sons, 1959.

GRAHAM, JOHN. *A Crowd of Cows.* Illustrated by Feodor Rojankovsky. New York: Harcourt, Brace & World, Inc., 1968.

GREET, W. CABELL, et al. *In Other Words: A Beginning Thesaurus.* Glenview, Ill.: Scott, Foresman & Co., 1968.

———. *Junior Thesaurus.* New York: Lothrop, Lee & Shepard Co., 1970.

HAUTZIG, ESTHER. *At Home: A Visit in Four Languages.* Illustrated by Aliki. New York: The Macmillan Company, 1968.

———. *In the Park: An Excursion in Four Languages.* Illustrated by Ezra Jack Keats. New York: The Macmillan Company, 1968.

HELFMAN, ELIZABETH S. *Signs and Symbols around the World.* New York: Lothrop, Lee & Shepard Co., 1967.

HOBAN, RUSSELL. *The Pedaling Man and Other Poems.* New York: W. W. Norton & Co., Inc., 1968.

HUBBELL, PATRICIA. *Catch Me a Wind.* Drawings by Susan Trommler. New York: Atheneum Publishers, 1968.

JOSLIN, SESYLE. *The Night They Stole the Alphabet.* Illustrated by Enrico Arno. New York: Harcourt, Brace & World, Inc., 1968.

JUSTER, NORTON. *The Phantom Tollbooth.* Illustrated by Jules Feiffer. New York: Random House, Inc., 1961.

KAMM, HERBERT, ed. *The Junior Illustrated Encyclopedia of Sports.* Illustrated by Willard Mullin. Indianapolis: The Bobbs-Merrill Co., Inc., 1970.

KAUFMAN, HOEL. *The Golden Book of Happy Words.* Racine, Wis.: Golden Press, Western Publishing Co., 1963.

KILIAN, CRAWFORD. *Wonders, Inc.* Illustrated by John Larrecq. Berkeley, Calif.: Parnassus Press, 1968. Grades 3-5.

KRAUSS, RUTH. *A Hole Is to Dig.* Illustrated by Maurice Sendak. New York: Harper & Row, Publishers, 1952.

LAIRD, HELENE AND CHARLTON. *The Tree of Language.* Cleveland: The World Publishing Co., 1957.

LAMBERT, ELOISE. *Our Language: The Story of the Words We Use.* New York: Lothrop, Lee & Shepard Co., 1955.

LIONNI, LEO. *The Alphabet Tree.* Illustrated by Leo Lionni. New York: Pantheon Books, 1968.

LONGMAN, HAROLD S. *What's Behind the Word?* Illustrated by Susan Perl. New York: Coward-McCann, Inc., 1968.

LUDOVICI, LAWRENCE JAMES. *Origins of Language.* Illustrated by Raymond Ludovici. (Science Survey Series.) New York: G. P. Putnam's Sons, 1965.

MATHEWS, MITFORD M. *American Words.* New York: The World Publishing Co., 1959.

MATTHIESEN, THOMAS. *ABC: An Alphabet Book.* Photographs by Thomas Matthiesen. Bronx, N.Y.: The Platt & Munk Co., Inc., 1966.

———. *Things to See.* Photographs by Thomas Matthiesen. Bronx, N.Y.: The Platt & Munk Co., Inc., 1966.

MERRIAM, EVE. *It Doesn't Always Have to Rhyme.* New York: Atheneum Publishers, 1964.

———. *A Gaggle of Geese.* New York: Alfred A. Knopf, Inc., 1960.

———. *Small Fry.* Illustrated by Garry MacKenzie. New York: Alfred A. Knopf, Inc., 1965.

MOORHOUSE, ALFRED C. *The Triumph of the Alphabet: A History of Writing.* New York: Abelard-Schuman, Ltd., 1953.

NURNBERG, MAXWELL W. *Wonders in Words*. Illustrated by Fred Turton. Englewood Cliffs, N.J.: Prentice-Hall, Inc., 1968.

OGG, OSCAR. *The 26 Letters*. Illustrated by Oscar Ogg. New York: Thomas Y. Crowell Co., 1961.

O'NEILL, MARY. *Take a Number*. Illustrated by Al Nagy. Garden City, N.Y.: Doubleday & Co., Inc., 1968.

———. *Words, Words, Words*. Illustrated by Judy Puissi-Campbell. Garden City, N.Y.: Doubleday & Co., Inc., 1966.

PARRISH, PEGGY. *Come Back, Amelia Bedelia*. New York: Harper & Row, Publishers, 1970. Grades Ps-3.

PEL, MARIO. *All About Language*. Philadelphia: J. B. Lippincott Co., 1954.

PROVENSEN, ALICE AND MARTIN. *Karen's Opposites*. Racine, Wis.: Golden Press, Western Publishing Co., 1963.

RADLAUER, RUTH S. *Good Times with Words*. Chicago: Melmont Publishers, Inc., 1963.

RAND, ANN AND PAUL. *I Know a Lot of Things*. Illustrated by Paul Rand. New York: Harcourt, Brace & World, Inc., 1956.

———. *Sparkle and Spin*. New York: Harcourt, Brace & World, Inc., 1957.

REID, ALASTAIR, *Ounce, Dice, Trice*. Illustrated by Ben Shawn. Boston: Atlantic Monthly Press, Little, Brown & Co., 1958.

ROSSNER, JUDITH. *What Kind of Feet Does a Bear Have?* Indianapolis: The Bobbs-Merrill Co., Inc., 1963.

RUSSELL, SOLVEIG P. *A Is for Apple and Why*. Nashville: Abingdon Press, 1959.

SAGE, MICHAEL. *Words Inside Words*. Philadelphia: J. B. Lippincott Co., 1961.

SELZ, IRMA. *Wonderful, Nice*. New York: Lothrop, Lee & Shepard, 1960. Grades K-4.

SEVERN, WILLIAM. *People Words*. New York: Ives Washburn, Inc., 1966.

SHIPLEY, JOSEPH T. *Word Games for Play and Power*. Englewood Cliffs, N.J.: Prentice-Hall, 1962.

———. *Playing With Words*. Englewood Cliffs, N.J.: Prentice-Hall, 1960.

———. *Dictionary of Word Origins*. Totowa, N.J.: Littlefield, Adams & Co., 1955.

SIMON, NORMA. *What Do I Say?* Pictures by Joe Lasker. Chicago: Albert Whitman & Co., 1967.

STEWART, GEORGE R. *Names on the Land*. rev. ed. Boston: Houghton Mifflin Co., 1958.

STOLZ, MARY. *Say Something*. Illustrated by Edward Frascino. New York: Harper & Row, Publishers, 1968.

STUART, JESSE. *A Penny's Worth of Character*. New York: McGraw-Hill Book Co., 1954. Grades 3-5.

TRESSELT, ALVIN. *Hide and Seek Fog*. Illustrated by Roger Duvoisin. New York: Lothrop, Lee & Shepard Co., 1965.

WALLER, LESLIE. *Our American Language*. New York: Holt, Rinehart & Winston, 1960.

WARBURG, SANDOL STODDARD. *Ambledee to Zumbledee*. Illustrated by Walter Lorraine. Boston: Houghton Mifflin Co., 1968.

WHITE, MARY S. *Word Twins*. Nashville: Abingdon Press, 1961.

WILDSMITH, BRIAN. *Brian Wildsmith's Fishes*. Illustrated by Brian Wildsmith. New York: Franklin Watts, 1968.

———. *Brian Wildsmith's 1, 2, 3's*. Illustrated by Brian Wildsmith. New York: Franklin Watts, 1965.

ZIM, HERBERT S. *Codes and Secret Writing*. New York: William Morrow & Co., 1948.

WRITTEN EXPRESSION

KOHN, BERNICE. *Secret Codes and Ciphers*. Illustrated by Frank Aloise. Englewood Cliffs, N.J.: Prentice-Hall, 1968. Grades 4-7.

KRAUSS, RUTH. *I Write It.* Illustrated by Mary Chalmers. New York: Harper & Row, Publishers, 1970. Grades Ps-1.

MAHON, JULIA. *The First Book of Creative Writing.* Illustrated by G. E. Nebel. New York: Franklin Watts, 1968. Grades 5-8.

ANIMALS

ANDERSON, SYDNEY. *The Lives of Animals.* Creative Education, 1965. Grades 5-7.

BERRILL, JACQUELINE. *Wonders of Animal Nurseries.* Illustrated by author. New York: Dodd, Mead & Co., 1968. Grades 3-5.

BLOUGH, GLENN O., AND CAMPBELL, MARJORIE H. *When You Go to the Zoo.* Illustrated. New York: McGraw-Hill, 1955. Grades 4-6.

BOWMAN, JOHN. *On Guard; Living Things Defend Themselves.* Illustrated by Howard Berelson. Garden City, N.Y.: Doubleday & Co., 1969. Grades Ps-5.

COHEN, DANIEL. *Animals of the City.* Drawings and photographs by Kiyoaki Komoda. New York: Mc-Graw-Hill Book Co., 1969. Grades 3-7.

FREEDMAN, RUSSELL, AND MORRISS, JAMES E. *How Animals Learn.* Illustrated with photographs. New York: Holiday House, 1969. Grades 4 and up.

GRABIANSKI, JANUSZ. *Dogs.* New York: Franklin Watts, Inc., 1968. Grades Ps-3.

KIRN, ANN. *Let's Look at Tracks.* Illustrated by author. New York: G. P. Putnam's Sons, 1969. Grades K-4.

LESKOWITZ, IRVING, AND STONE, A. HARRIS. *Animals Are Like This.* Illustrated by Peter P. Plasencia. Englewood Cliffs, N.J.: Prentice-Hall, Inc., 1968. Grades 4-7.

MASON, G. F. *Animal Habits.* Illustrated. New York: William Morrow & Co., 1959. Grades 4-6.

———. *Animal Homes.* Illustrated. New York: William Morrow & Co., 1947. Grades 4-6.

MASON, ROBERT G., ed. *The Life Picture Book of Animals.* Illustrated. New York: Time, Inc., Books Division, 1969.

SANDER, LENORE. *Animals that Work for Man.* Illustrated by Polly Bolian. Englewood Cliffs, N.J.: Prentice-Hall, 1963. Grades 3-6.

SELSAM, MILLICENT E. *Animals as Parents.* Illustrated by John Kaufmann. New York: William Morrow & Co., Inc., 1965. Grades 5-7.

———. *How Animals Tell Time.* Illustrated by Kathleen Elgin. New York: William Morrow & Co., 1967.

———. *The Language of Animals.* Illustrated by Kathleen Elgin. New York: William Morrow & Co., 1962. Grades 4-6.

SIMON, SEYMOUR. *Discovering What Frogs Do.* Illustrated by Jean Zallinger. New York: McGraw-Hill Book Co., Inc., 1969. Grades 2-6.

SUTTON, ANN AND MYRON. *Animals on the Move.* Illustrated by Paula A. Hutchinson. Skokie, Ill.: Rand McNally & Co., 1965. Grades 3-6.

VAN FRISCH, OTTO. *Animal Migrations.* Illustrated. New York: McGraw-Hill Book Co., Inc., 1969. Grades 5 and up.

BIOGRAPHY

BAUMANN, HANS. *Alexander's Great March.* Translated by Stella Humphries. New York: Henry Z. Walck, Inc., 1968. Grades 6-8.

GIBLAND, EILEEN. *Queen Elizabeth I.* New York: Criterion Books, Inc., 1965. Grades 7 and up.

BONTEMPS, ARNA. *Frederick Douglass: Slave-Fighter-Freeman.* Illustrated by Harper Johnson. New York: Alfred A. Knopf, Inc., 1959. Grades 5-7.

COIT, MARGARET. *Andrew Jackson.* Illustrated by Milton Johnson. Boston: Houghton Mifflin Co., 1965.

DALGLIESCH, ALICE. *The Columbus Story.* Illustrated by Leo Politi. New York: Charles Scribner's Sons, 1955. Grades 1-4.

DAUGHERTY, JAMES. *Daniel Boone.* New York: The Viking Press, Inc., 1939. Grades 4-6.

D'AULAIRE, INGRI AND EDGAR P. *Abraham Lincoln.* Illustrated by authors. Garden City, N. Y.: Doubleday & Co., Inc., 1939; 1957. Grades 2-5.

DEGERING, ETTA. *Seeing Fingers: The Story of Louis Braille.* Illustrated by Emil Weiss. New York: David McKay Co., Inc., 1962. Grades 5-7.

EPSTEIN, SAMUEL, AND EPSTEIN, BERYL (WILLIAMS). *Harriet Tubman: Guide to Freedom.* Illustrated by Paul Frame. Scarsdale, N.Y.: Garrard Publishing Co., 1968. Grades 3-5.

FISHER, AILEEN LUCIA, AND RABE, OLIVE. *We Alcotts; the Story of Louisa M. Alcott's Family as Seen through the Eyes of "Marmee," Mother of Little Women.* Decorations by Ellen Raskin. New York: Atheneum Publishers, 1968. Grades 5-8.

FORBES, ESTHER. *America's Paul Revere.* Illustrated by Lynd Ward. Boston: Houghton Mifflin Co., 1946. Grades 5-9.

GREGOR, ARTHUR. *Galileo.* Illustrated by George Giusti. New York: Charles Scribner's Sons, 1965. Grades 3-7.

HEDERSTADT, DOROTHY. *Frontier Leaders and Pioneers.* Illustrated by Clifford N. Geary. New York: David McKay Co., Inc., 1962. Grades 5-7.

HENRY, MARGUERITE. *Benjamin West and His Cat Grimalkin.* Illustrated by Wesley Dennis. Indianapolis: Bobbs-Merrill Co., 1947. Grades 4-6.

JOHNSTON, JOHANNA. *A Special Bravery.* Illustrated by Ann Grifalconi. New York: Dodd, Mead & Co., 1967. Grades 2-5.

JUDSON, CLARA I. *City Neighbor: The Story of Jane Addams.* Illustrated by Ralph Ray. New York: Charles Scribner's Sons, 1951. Grades 5-7.

KYLE, ELISABETH. *Great Ambitions: A Story of the Early Years of Charles Dickens.* New York: Holt, Rinehart & Winston, n.d.

LATHAM, JEAN LEE. *Anchor's Aweigh; The Story of David Glasgow Farragut.* Illustrated by Eros Keith. New York: Harper & Row, Publishers, 1968. Grades 5-8.

LAWSON, ROBERT. *They Were Strong and Good.* Illustrated by author. New York: The Viking Press, Inc., 1940. Grades 4-6.

LISS, HOWARD. *The Making of a Rookie.* Glossary of Pro Football Terms. New York: Random House, 1968. Grades 6-9.

LOMASK, MILTON. *John Quincy Adams.* New York: Farrar, Straus & Giroux, 1965.

MANN, PEGGY. *Clara Barton, Battlefield Nurse.* Pictures by Angie Culfogienis. New York: Coward-McCann, 1969. Grades 3-5.

MARTIN, PATRICIA MILES. *John Fitzgerald Kennedy.* Illustrated by Paul Frame. New York: G. P. Putnam's Sons, 1964. Grades 2-4.

MEIGS, CORNELIA LYNDE. *Invincible Louisa; The Story of the Author of Little Women.* Illustrations. Boston: Little, Brown & Co., 1968. Grades 6-9.

MILLENDER, DHARATHULA. *Crispus Attucks: Boy of Valor.* Indianapolis: Bobbs-Merrill Co. Grades 3-5.

MONTGOMERY, ELIZABETH RIDER. *William C. Handy; Father of the Blues.* Illustrated by David Hodges. Scarsdale N.Y.: Garrard Publishing Co., 1968. Grades 3-6.

PEARE, CATHERINE O. *The Helen Keller Story.* New York: Thomas Y. Crowell Co., 1959. Grades 5-7.

PRESTON, EDWARD. *Martin Luther King: Fighter for Freedom.* Garden City, N.Y.: Doubleday & Co., 1969. Grades 8 and up.

SCHULTZ, PEARLE HENRIKSEN. *Sir Walter Scott: Wizard of the North.* New York: Vanguard Press, n.d.

SMARIDGE, NORAH. *Famous Modern Storytellers for Young People.* Photographs. New York: Dodd, Mead & Co., 1969. Grades 7-11.

STOUTENBURG, ADRIEN, AND BAKER, LAURA NELSON. *Listen America: A Life of Walt Whitman.* New York: Charles Scribner's Sons, n.d.

SULLIVAN, WILSON (and the eds. of American Heritage). *Franklin Delano Roosevelt.* New York: American Heritage; Harper & Row, Publishers, 1970. Grades 6 and up.

SYME, RONALD. *Amerigo Vespucci, Scientist and Sailor.* Illustrated by William Stobbs. New York: William Morrow & Co., 1969. Grades 5-7.

———. *Bolivar the Liberator.* Illustrated by William Stobbs. New York: William Morrow & Co., 1968. Grades 4-6.

DE TREVINO, ELIZABETH BORTON. *I, Juan de Pareja.* New York: Farrar, Straus & Giroux, 1965.

VAETH, JOSEPH GORDON. *The Man Who Founded Georgia.* New York: Crowell Collier & Macmillan Co., 1968. Grades 6-9.

VEGLAHN, NANCY. *Peter Cartwright, Pioneer Circuit Rider.* New York: Charles Scribner's Sons, 1968. Grades 6-9.

WENTWORTH, ELAINE. *Mission to Metlakatla.* Boston: Houghton Mifflin Co., 1968. Grades 5-8.

WILLIAMS, JAY. *Leonardo da Vinci.* New York: American Heritage Publishing Co., 1965.

WOOD, JAMES PLAYSTED. *Spunkwater, Spunkwater! A Life of Mark Twain.* New York: Pantheon Books, n.d.

WYATT, EDGAR. *Cochise: Apache Warrior and Statesman.* Illustrated by Allan Houser. New York: McGraw-Hill Book Co., 1953. Grades 4-6.

BIRDS

AUSTIN, ELIZABETH S. *Penguins: The Birds with Flippers.* Illustrations, col. map. New York: Random House, 1968. Grades 4-6.

BLOUGH, GLENN O. *Bird Watchers and Bird Feeders.* Illustrated by Jeanne Bendick. New York: McGraw-Hill Book Co., 1963. Grades 1-3.

EARLE, OLIVE L. *Birds of the Crow Family.* Illustrated by author. New York: William Morrow & Co., 1962. Grades 3-4.

EIMERL, SAREL. *Gulls.* Photographs. New York: Simon & Schuster, 1969. Grades 1-5.

FENTON, CARROLL, AND PALLAS, DOROTHY. *Birds and Their World.* Illustrated by Carroll Fenton. New York: John Day Co., 1954. Grades 4-6.

FENTON, CARROLL LANE, AND KITCHEN, HERMINIE B. *Birds We Live With.* Illustrated by Carroll L. Fenton. New York: John Day Co., 1963. Grades 4-6.

GRABIANSKI, JANUSZ. *Birds.* Illustrations. New York: Franklin Watts, 1968. Grades Ps-3.

KAUFMANN, JOHN. *Wings, Sun, and Stars; The Story of Bird Migration.* Illustrated by author. New York: William Morrow & Co., 1969. Grades 5-9.

McCLUNG, ROBERT. *Honker: The Story of a Wild Goose.* New York: William Morrow & Co., 1965. Grades 3-6.

McCOY, JOSEPH J. *House Sparrows, Ragamuffins of the City.* Drawings by Jean Zallinger. New York: Seabury Press, 1968. Grades 3-6.

REED, GWENDOLYN E., comp. *Bird Songs.* Drawings by Gabriele Margules. New York: Atheneum Publishers, 1969. Grades 5-8.

SEARS, PAUL M. *Barn Swallow.* Illustrated by Walter Ferguson. New York: Holiday House, 1955. Grades 3-6.

SIMON, HILDA. *Wonders of Hummingbirds.* Illustrated by author. New York: Dodd, Mead & Co., 1964. Grades 4-6.

WELTY, SUSAN F. *Birds with Bracelets: The Story of Bird-Banding.* Illustrated by John Kaufmann. Englewood Cliffs, N.J.: Prentice-Hall, 1965. Grades 4-7.

WHITEHEAD, ROBERT J. *The First Book of Eagles*. Illustrated by Haris Petie. New York: Franklin Watts, 1968. Grades 5-7.

WILLIAMSON, MARGARET. *The First Book of Birds*. Illustrated by author. New York: Franklin Watts, 1951. Grades 4-6.

EARTH, SKY, AND SPACE

AMES, GERALD, AND WYLER, ROSE. *Planet Earth*. Illustrated by Cornelius DeWitt. Racine, Wis.: Golden Press, Western Publishing Co., 1963. Grades 6-8.

ARCHER, SELLERS G. *Rain, Rivers and Reservoirs: The Challenge of Running Water*. Illustrated with maps and photographs. New York: Coward-McCann, 1963; 1969. Grades 5-7.

ASIMOV, ISAAC. *Galaxies*. Paintings by Alex Ebel and Denny McManus. Chicago: Follett Publishing Co., 1968. Grades 2-4.

BEHNKE, FRANCES. *What We Find When We Look under Rocks*. Three-color drawings by Catherine Hanley. New York: McGraw-Hill Book Co., 1969. Grades 1-4.

BENDICK, JEANNE. *Space and Time*. Illustrated by author. New York: Franklin Watts, 1968. Grades 2-4.

BERGAUST, ERIK. *The Russians in Space*. Illustrations. New York: G. P. Putnam's Sons, 1969. Grades 5-9.

BLACK, IRMA S. *Busy Water*. Illustrated. New York: Holiday House, 1958. Grades 2-4.

BRANLEY, FRANKLYN M. *A Book of Stars for You*. Illustrated by Leonard Kessler. New York: Thomas Y. Crowell Co., 1967. Grades 3-5.

BRINDZE, RUTH. *The Story of Our Calendar*. Illustrated by Helene Carter. New York: Vanguard Press, 1949. Grades 4-8.

BURT, OLIVE. *The First Book of Salt*. Illustrated with photographs. New York: Franklin Watts, 1965. Grades 4-6.
Watts, 1965. Grades 4-6.

ELTING, MARY. *Spacecraft at Work*. rev. ed. Illustrated by Ursula Koering. Irvington-on-Hudson, N.Y.: Harvey House, 1966.

FARB, PETER. *The Story of Dams: An Introduction to Hydrology*. Illustrated by George Kanelous. Irvington-on-Hudson, N.Y.: Harvey House, 1961. Grades 5-7.

FENTON, CARROLL, AND FENTON, MILDRED A. *Worlds in the Sky*. Illustrated by authors. New York: John Day Co., 1963. Grades 4-6.

FERAVOLO, ROCCO V. *Around the World in Ninety Minutes; The Journey of Two Astronauts*. Illustrated by William Steinel. New York: Lothrop, Lee & Shepard Co., 1968. Grades 1-4.

GALLANT, ROY A. *Exploring Mars*. rev. ed. Illustrated by Lowell Hess. Garden City, N.Y.: Doubleday & Co., 1968. Grades 4-7.

GOETZ, DELIA. *Rivers*. Illustrated by John Kaufmann. New York: William Morrow & Co., 1969. Grades 3-7.

GOODHEART, BARBARA. *A Year on the Desert*. Illustrated by Mel Hunter. Englewood Cliffs, N.J.: Prentice-Hall, 1969. Grades 5 and up.

GRISSOM, VIRGIL I. *Gemini; A Personal Account of Man's Venture into Space*. Illustrated. New York: Macmillan Co., 1968.

HEADY, ELEANOR B. *Coat of the Earth; The Story of Grass*. Drawings by Harold F. Heady. New York: W. W. Norton & Co., 1968. Grades 5-8.

IVINS, ANN. *Stars and Constellations*. Illustrated by Robert Galandak. New York: Crowell Collier & Macmillan Co., 1969. Grades 1-4.

KNIGHT, DAVID C. *Comets*. Illustrated. New York: Franklin Watts, 1968. Grades 5-8.

LAUBER, PATRICIA. *Big Dreams and Small Rockets: A Short History of Space Travel*. Illustrated with photographs. New York: Thomas Y. Crowell Co., 1965. Grades 5-7.

LEY, WILLY. *Inside the Orbit of the Earth.* Illustrated with charts and line drawings by Rino Dussi. New York: McGraw-Hill Book Co., 1968. Grades 6-9.

————. *The Gas Giants; The Largest Planets.* With line drawings. New York: McGraw-Hill Book Co., 1969. Grades 5 and up.

MARSHALL, JAMES. *The Air We Live in; Air Pollution: What We Must Do about It.* Consultant: Matthew Brennan. New York: Coward-McCann, 1969. Grades 6-9.

NEWELL, HOMER EDWARD. *Space Book for Young People.* Illustrated by Anne Marie Jauss. New York: McGraw-Hill Book Co., 1968. Grades 7-9.

OLDS, ELIZABETH. *Deep Treasure.* Illustrated. Boston: Houghton Mifflin Co., 1958. Grades 3-5.

QUILICI, FOLCO. *The Great Deserts.* Adapted by Margaret O. Hyde. Illustrated. New York: McGraw-Hill Book Co., 1969. Grades 5 and up.

SASEK, M. *This is Cape Kennedy.* Illustrated by author. New York: Macmillan Co., 1964. Grades 2-5.

SCHNEIDER, HERMAN AND NINA. *Rocks, Rivers, and the Changing Earth.* Illustrated by Edwin Herron. New York: William R. Scott, 1952. Grades 5-8.

————. *You Among the Stars.* Illustrated by Symeon Shimin. New York: William R. Scott, 1951. Grades 3-5.

SCHNEIDER, LEO. *Space in Your Future.* Illustrated. New York: Harcourt, Brace & World, 1961. Grades 4-6.

SHELTON, WILLIAM ROY. *American Space Exploration; The First Decade.* Boston: Little, Brown & Co., 1967.

SHUTTLESWORTH, DOROTHY EDWARDS. *Clean Air, Sparkling Water; The Fight Against Pollution.* Illustrated. Garden City, N.Y.: Doubleday & Co., 1968. Grades 3-5.

SIMON, SEYMOUR. *Wet and Dry.* Illustrated by Angeline V. Culfogienis. New York: McGraw-Hill Book Co., 1969. Grades Ps-3.

SMITH, FRANCES. *The First Book of Mountains.* Illustrated. New York: Franklin Watts, 1964. Grades 4-6.

SMITH, FRANCES C. *The First Book of Conservation.* Illustrated by Rene Martin. New York: Franklin Watts, 1954. Grades 4-6.

TALLEY, NAOMI. *To Save the Soil.* Illustrated. New York: Dial Press, 1965. Grades 4-6.

WHITE, ANNE TERRY. *All About Mountains.* Illustrated with photographs. New York: Random House, 1962. Grades 5-7.

WYLER, ROSE, AND AMES, GERALD. *The New Golden Book of Astronomy.* Illustrated by John Polgreed. Racine, Wis.: Golden Press, Western Publishing Co., 1955. Grades 5-9.

ZIM, HERBERT S. *What's Inside the Earth?* Illustrated by Raymond Perlman, New York: William Morrow & Co., 1953. Grades 4-9.

————. *The Universe.* Illustrated by Gustav Schrotter. New York: William Morrow & Co., 1958. Grades 4-6.

————. *Shooting Stars.* Illustrated by Gustav Schrotter. New York: William Morrow & Co., 1958. Grades 4-7.

ENERGY AND POWER

ADLER, IRVING AND RUTH. *Atoms and Molecules.* New York: John Day Co., 1966. Grades 3-6.

————. *Magnets.* New York: John Day Co., 1966. Grades 4-6.

BRONOWSKI, J. AND SELSAM, MILLICENT E. *Biography of an Atom.* Illustrated by Weimer Pursell and with photographs. New York: Harper & Row, Publishers, 1965. Grades 4-7.

EPSTEIN, SAM AND BERYL. *The First Book of Electricity.* Illustrated with photographs. New York: Franklin Watts, 1953; 1966. Grades 4-7.

FERMI LAURA. *The Story of Atomic Energy.* New York: Random House, 1961. Grades 5-9.

FREEMAN, IRA MAXIMILIAN. *Light and Radiation.* Illustrated by George T. Resch. New York: Random House, 1969. Grades 5-8.

HOGBEN, LANCELOT THOMAS. *The Wonderful World of Energy.* Garden City, N.Y.: Doubleday & Co., 1968. Grades 6-9.

IRVING, ROBERT. *Energy and Power.* Illustrated by Leonard Everett Fisher. New York: Alfred A. Knopf, 1958. Grades 4-7.

LIEBERG, OWEN S. *Wonders of Heat and Light.* Illustrated with photographs by author. New York: Dodd, Mead & Co., 1966. Grades 5-7.

SCHNEIDER, HERMAN AND NINA. *More Power to You.* Illustrated by Bill Ballentine. New York: William R. Scott.

VALENS, E. G. *Magnet.* Photographs by Bernice Abbott. Cleveland: World Publishing Co., 1964. Grades 5-7.

———. *Motion.* Illustrated with photographs by Bernice Abbott. Cleveland: World Publishing Co., 1965. Grades 4-6.

ENGINEERING AND HOW THINGS WORK

ALEXANDER, ANNE. *ABC of Cars and Trucks.* Garden City, N.Y.: Doubleday & Co., 1956. Grades K-3.

BATE, NORMAN. *Who Built the Dam?* Illustrated by author. New York: Charles Scribner's Sons, 1958. Grades 3-5.

BRADLEY, DUANE. *Engineers Did It!* Illustrated by Anne Marie Jauss. Philadelphia: J. B. Lippincott Co., 1958. Grades 3-5.

COOKE, DAVID C. *How Automobiles Are Made.* Illustrated. New York: Dodd, Mead & Co., 1957. Grades 4-6.

CORBETT, SCOTT. *What Makes a Car Go?* Illustrated by Len Darwin. Boston: Little, Brown & Co., 1963. Grades 2-3.

———. *What Makes TV Work?* Illustrated by Len Darwin. Boston: Little, Brown & Co., 1965. Grades 4-6.

FLACK, MARJORIE. *The Boats on the River.* Illustrated by Jay Hyde Barnum. New York: Viking Press, 1946. Grades K-3.

GOLDWATER, DANIEL. *Bridges and How They Are Built.* Illustrated by Harvey Weiss. New York: William R. Scott, 1965. Grades 5-7.

HEINTZE, CARL. *A Million Locks and Keys, The Story of Immunology.* Illustrated with photographs and drawings. Des Moines: Meredith Corp., 1969. Grades 5 and up.

HELFMAN, ELIZABETH S. *Wheels, Scoops, and Buckets; How People Lift Water for Their Fields.* Illustrated by Eva Cellini. New York: Lothrop, Lee & Shepard Co., 1968. Grades 3-5.

HIRSCH, S. CARL. *This Is Automation.* Illustrated by Anthony Ravielli. New York: Viking Press, 1964. Grades 5-6.

IGER, MARTIN AND EVE MARIE. *Building a Skyscraper.* Photographs by Martin Iger. New York: William R. Scott, 1967. Grades 5-7.

KOHN, BERNICE. *Telephones.* Illustrated by Joseph Low. New York: Coward-McCann, 1967. Grades 2-3.

MEYER, JEROME. *Machines.* Illustrated. Cleveland: World Publishing Co., 1958. Grades 4-8.

MORGAN, ALFRED. *The Boys' Fourth Book of Radio and Electronics.* Illustrated with diagrams by author. New York: Charles Scribner's Sons, 1969. Grades 7-11.

NORDNER, WILLIAM. *Model Ships.* Illustrated with drawings. Des Moines: Meredith Corp., 1969. Grades 5 and up.

NORRIS, GUNILLA. *A Time for Watching*. Illustrated by Paul Giovanopoulos. New York: Alfred A. Knopf, 1969. Grades 3-7.

OLNEY, ROSS R. *Sound All Around: How Hi-Fi and Stereo Work*. Illustrated by Lewis Zacks. Englewood Cliffs, N.J.: Prentice-Hall, 1967. Grades 4-6.

PRATT, FLETCHER. *All About Famous Inventors and Their Inventions*. Illustrated. New York: Random House, 1957. Grades 4-7.

SCHNEIDER, HERMAN AND NINA. *Your Telephone and How It Works*. Illustrated by Jeanne Bendick. New York: McGraw-Hill Book Co., 1952; 1965. Grades 5-9.

STIRLING, NORA B. *Wonders of Engineering*. Illustrated by Emil Weiss. Garden City, N.Y.: Doubleday & Co., 1966. Grades 4-7.

VEGLAHN, NANCY. *The Spider of Brooklyn Heights*. Illustrated. New York: Charles Scribner's Sons, 1967. Grades 5-7.

WEISS, HARVEY. *Motors and Engines and How They Work*. Illustrated. New York: Thomas Y. Crowell Co., 1969. Grades 5-8.

WOOLLEY, CATHERINE. *I Like Trains*. Illustrated by George Fonseca. New York: Harper & Row, Publishers, 1944; 1965. Grades Ps-1.

YOUNG, MIRIAM. *If I Drove a Truck*. Illustrated by Robert Quackenbush. New York: Lothrop, Lee & Shepard Co., 1967. Grades Ps-1.

ZAFFO, GEORGE J. *The Big Book of Real Fire Engines*. Illustrated by author. New York: Grosset & Dunlap, 1950; 1964. Grades 1-4.

ZIM, HERBERT SPENCER, AND SKELLEY, JAMES R. *Machine Tools*. Illustrated by Gary Ruse. New York: William Morrow & Co., Grades 3-6.

ZIM, HERBERT S. *What's Inside of Engines?* Illustrated by Raymond Perlman. New York: William Morrow & Co., 1953. Grades 4-7.

EXPERIMENTS

BARR, GEORGE. *Fun and Tricks for Young Scientists*. Illustrated by Mildred Waltrip. New York: McGraw-Hill Book Co., 1968. Grades 5-7.

———. *Research Ideas for Young Scientists*. Illustrated by John Teppich. New York: McGraw-Hill Book Co., 1958. Grades 5 and up.

FENTEN, D. X. *Plants for Pots; Projects for Indoor Gardeners*. Illustrated by Penelope Naylor. Philadelphia: J. B. Lippincott Co., 1969. Grades 5-9.

FERAVOLO, ROCCO V. *More Easy Physics Projects; Magnetism, Electricity, Sound*. Illustrated by Marvin Besunder. Englewood Cliffs, N.J.: Prentice-Hall, 1968. Grades 4-7.

FREEMAN, MAE (BLACKER). *The Book of Magnets*. Pictures by Norman Bridwell. New York: Four Winds Press, Scholastic Book Services, 1968. Grades 1-4.

HARBECK, RICHARD. *Exploring Science in Your Home Laboratory*. Illustrated with photographs. New York: Four Winds Press, Scholastic Book Services, 1965. Grades 5-7.

HEADSTROM, RICHARD. *Adventures with a Hand Lens*. Illustrated by author. Philadelphia: J. B. Lippincott Co., 1962. Grades 5-8.

KNIGHT, DAVID C. *The First Book of Sound*. Illustrated. New York: Franklin Watts, 1960. Grades 4-6.

MILGROM, HARRY. *Adventures with a Paper Cup*. Illustrated by Leonard Kessler. New York: E. P. Dutton & Co., 1968. Grades Ps-2.

MORGAN, ALFRED POWELL. *First Chemistry Book for Boys and Girls*. New York: Charles Scribner's Sons, 1950. Grades 5-7.

RASKIN, EDITH. *The Fantastic Cactus; Indoors and in Nature*. Illustrated. New York: Lothrop, Lee & Shepard Co., 1968. Grades 5-9.

SCHNEIDER, NINA AND HERMAN. *Let's Find Out*. Illustrated by Jeanne Bendick. New York: William R. Scott, 1946. Grades 3-6.

SCHWARTZ, JULIUS. *It's Fun to Know Why: Experiments with Things around Us.* Illustrated by Edwin Herron. New York: McGraw-Hill Book Co., 1952. Grades 4-6.

SIMON, SEYMOUR. *Animals in Field and Laboratory: Science Projects in Animal Behavior.* Illustrated by Emily McCully. New York: McGraw-Hill Book Co., 1968. Grades 4 and up.

STONE, A. HARRIS, AND INGMANSON, DALE. *Drop by Drop: A Look at Water.* Illustrated by Peter P. Plasencia. Englewood Cliffs, N.J.: Prentice-Hall, 1969. Grades 4-7.

STONE, A. HARRIS, AND SIEGAL, BERTRAM M. *The Chemistry of Soap.* Illustrated by Peter P. Plasencia. Englewood Cliffs, N.J.: Prentice-Hall, 1968. Grades 4-7.

YATES, RAYMOND. *The Boys' Book of Magnetism.* New York: Harper & Row, Publishers, 1959. Grades 4-7.

FOLKTALES, FAIRY TALES, AND LEGENDS

ALGER, LECLAIRE. *Sea-Spell and Moor-Magic; Tales of the Western Isles, by Sorche Nic Leodhas.* Illustrated by Vera Bock. New York: Holt, Rinehart & Winston, 1968. Grades 4-7.

ARTZYBASHEFF, BORIS. *Seven Simeons: A Russian Tale.* Illustrated by author. New York: Viking Press, 1961. Grades 4-6.

ASBJORNSEN, PETER C., AND MOE, J. E., comps. *East of the Sun and West of the Moon.* New York: Macmillan Co., 1969. Grades K-5.

———. *Norwegian Folk Tales.* New York: Viking Press, 1969. Grades K-5.

———. *East of the Sun and West of the Moon; Twenty-one Norwegian Folk Tales.* Ed. and illustrated by Ingri and Edgar Parin d'Aulaire. New York: Viking Press, 1969. Grades 3-6.

BAKER, AUGUSTA, ed. *The Golden Lynx and Other Tales.* Illustrated by Johannes Troyer. Philadelphia: J. B. Lippincott Co., 1960. Grades 4-6.

BELPRE, PURA. *Ote, A Puerto Rican Tale.* Pictures by Paul Galdone. New York: Pantheon Books, 1969. Grades Ps-3.

BELTING, NATALIA. *The Stars Are Silver Reindeer.* Illustrated by Esta Nesbitt. New York: Holt, Rinehart & Winston, 1966. Grades 4 and up.

CARLSON, NATALIE SAVAGE. *The Talking Cat and Other Stories of French Canada.* Illustrated by Roger Duvoisin. New York: Harper & Row, Publishers, 1952. Grades 1-6.

COLUM, PADRAIC. *Children of Odin.* New York: Macmillan Co., 1930; 1962. Grades 4-6.

COURLANDER, HAROLD, ed. *The King's Drum and other African Stories.* Illustrated by Enrico Arno. New York: Harcourt, Brace & World, 1962. Grades 4-6.

D'AULAIRE, INGRI AND EDGAR PARIN. *East of the Sun and West of the Moon.* Illustrated by authors. New York: Viking Press, 1969. Grades 3-7.

D'AULNOY, LACOMTESSE. *The White Can and other Old French Tales.* Arranged by Rachel Field. Illustrated by E. MacKinstry. New York: Macmillan Co., 1967. Grades 3-6.

DOMANSKA, JANINA. *The Turnip.* New York: Macmillan Co., 1969.

DURHAM, MAE. *Tit for Tat and other Latvian Folk Tales.* Illustrated by Harriet Pincus. New York: Harcourt, Brace & World, 1967. Grades 4-6.

FELTON, HAROLD W. *True Tall Tales of Stormalong: Sailor of the Seven Seas.* Illustrated by Joan Sandin. Englewood Cliffs, N.J.: Prentice-Hall, 1968. Grades 3-6.

GOBHAI, MEHLLI. *Usha, the Mouse-Maiden.* Retold and illustrated by author. New York: Hawthorn Books, 1969. Grades Ps-3.

GREEN, ROGER LANCELYN. *Tales of Ancient Egypt, Selected and Retold.* Illustrated by Elaine Raphael. New York: Henry Z. Walck, 1968. Grades 6-9.

GRIMM BROTHERS. *German Folk Tales.* Translated by Francis P. Magous, Jr. and Alexander H. Krappe. Southern Illinois University Press, 1969. Grades 3-5.

HARDENDORFF, JEANNE B., comp. *Just One More*. Retold. Illustrated by Don Golognese. Philadelphia: J. B. Lippincott Co., 1969. Grades 3-6.

HARMAN, HUMPHREY. *Tales Told Near a Crocodile: Stories from Nyanza*. Illustrated by George Ford. New York: Viking Press, 1967. Grades 3-6.

HEADY, ELEANOR B. *When the Stones Were Soft: East African Fireside Tales*. Illustrated by Tom Feelings. New York: Funk & Wagnalls, 1968. Grades 4-7.

ISH-KISHOR, SULAMITH. *The Carpet of Solomon: A Hebrew Legend*. Illustrated by Uri Shulevitz. New York: Pantheon Books, 1966. Grades 4-6.

JACOBS, JOSEPH, comp. *More English Fairy Tales*. Illustrated by John D. Batten. Schocken, 1968. Grades 4-6.

JEWETT, ELEANORE M. *Which Was Witch?* Illustrated by Taro Yashima. New York: Viking Press, 1953. Grades 4-6.

LANG, ANDREW, ed. *King Arthur; Tales of the Round Table*. Pictures by Charles Mozley. New York: Franklin Watts, 1968. Grades 5-7.

LEODHAS, SORCHE NIC. *Claymore and Kilt: Tales of Scottish Kings and Castles*. Illustrated by Leo and Diane Dillon. New York: Holt, Rinehart & Winston, 1967. Grades 4-7.

MACMANUS, SEUMAS. *Hibernian Nights*. Illustrated by Paul Kennedy. New York: Macmillan Co., 1963. Grades 4-6.

MANNING-SANDERS, RUTH. *Damian and the Dragon: Modern Greek Folk-Tales*. Illustrated by William Papas. New York: Roy Publishers, 1965. Grades 5-7.

———. *The Red King and the Witch: Gypsy Folk and Fairy Tales*. Illustrated by Victor G. Ambrus. New York: Roy Publishers, 1965. Grades 4-5.

MASEY, MARY LOU. *Stories of the Steppes; Kazakh Folktales*. Retold. Pictures by Helen Basilevsky. New York: David McKay Co., 1968. Grades 4-6.

MATSON, EMERSON N. *Longhouse Legends*. Illustrated by Lorence Bjorklund. Camden, N.J.: Thomas Nelson & Sons, 1968. Grades 4-6.

MATSUTANI, MIYOKO. *The Crane Maiden*. Illustrated by Chihiro Iwasaki. English version by Alvin Tresselt. New York: Parents' Magazine Press, 1968. Grades K-3.

MEHDEVI, ANNE SINCLAIR. *Persian Folk and Fairy Tales*. Illustrated by Paul E. Kennedy. New York: Alfred A. Knopf, 1965. Grades 4-6.

NEWCOMB, FRANC JOHNSON. *Navajo Bird Tales*. Illustrated by No-Ton-Sa-Ka. New York: Harlen Quist Books, 1970.

NEWMAN, ROBERT. *Grettir the Strong*. Retold. Illustrated by John Gretzer. New York: Thomas Y. Crowell Co., 1968. Grades 5-7.

NYBLOM, HELENA AUGUSTA (ROED). *The Witch of the Woods; Fairy Tales from Sweden*. Illustrated by Nils Christian Hald. Translated by Holger Lundbergh. New York: Alfred A. Knopf, 1968. Grades 4-6.

NYE, ROBERT. *Beowulf; A New Telling*. Illustrated by Alan E. Cober. New York: Hill & Wang, 1968. Grades 5-8.

O'SULLIVAN, SEAN, ed. *Folk Tales of Ireland*. Translated by author. Chicago: University of Chicago Press, 1969.

PICARD, BARBARA L. *The Lady of the Linden Tree*. Illustrated by Charles Stewart. New York: Criterion Books, 1962. Grades 4-6.

PUGH, ELLEN. *Tales from the Welsh Hills*. Illustrated by Joan Sandin. New York: Dodd, Mead & Co., 1968. Grades 4-6.

RANSOME, ARTHUR. *The Fool of the World and the Flying Ship; A Russian Tale*. Retold. Pictures by Uri Shulevitz. New York: Farrar, Straus & Giroux, 1968. Grades K-3.

ROCKWELL, ANNE F. *The Good Llama*. Illustrated by author. New York: World Publishing Co., 1968. Grades 1-4.

SECHRIST, ELIZABETH (HOUGH). *Once In the First Times; Folk Tales from the Phillipines*. Retold. Illustrated by John Sheppard. Philadelphia: Macrae Smith Co., 1969. Grades 4-6.

SEREDY, KATE. *The White Stag.* Illustrated by author. New York: Viking Press, 1937. Grades 5-9.

SERRAILLIER, IAN. *Robin in the Greenwood; Ballads of Robin Hood.* Illustrated by Victor G. Ambrus. New York: Henry Z. Walck, 1968. Grades 5-8.

SHEPPARD-JONES, ELIZABETH. *Welsh Legendary Tales.* Illustrated by Paul Hogarth. Camden, N.J.: Thomas Nelson & Sons, 1960. Grades 4-6.

SHERLOCK, SIR PHILIP MANDERSON. *The Iguana's Tail; Crick Crack Stories from the Caribbean.* Illustrated by Gioia Fiammenghi. New York: Thomas Y. Crowell Co., 1969. Grades 3-5..

SIDDIQUI, ASHRAF, AND LERCH, MARILYN. *Toontoony Pie and Other Tales from Pakistan.* Illustrated by Jan Fairservis. New York: World Publishing Co., 1961. Grades 4-6.

SINGER, ISAAC BASHEVIS. *The Fearsome Inn.* Illustrated by Nonny Hogrogian. New York: Charles Scribner's Sons, 1967. Grades 3-6.

———. *When Shlemiel Went to Warsaw, and Other Stories.* Pictures by Margot Zemach. Translated by author and Elizabeth Shub. New York: Farrar, Straus & Giroux, 1968. Grades 4-6.

SPELLMAN, JOHN W. *The Beautiful Blue Jay and Other Tales of India.* Illustrated by Jerry Pinkney. Boston: Little, Brown & Co., 1967. Grades 4-6.

STAMM, CLAUS. *Three Strong Women: A Tall Tale from Japan.* Illustrated by Kazue Mizumura. New York: Viking Press, 1962, Grades 3-5.

TASHJIAN, VIRGINIA A. *Once There Was and Was Not: Armenian Tales.* Retold. Illustrated by Nonny Hogragian. Boston: Little, Brown & Co., 1966.

THOMPSON, STITH. *One Hundred Favorite Folktales.* Bloomington, Ind.: Indiana University Press, 1969.

TRAVEN, B. *The Creation of the Sun and the Moon.* Illustrated by Alberto Beltran. New York: Hill & Wang, 1968. Grades 4-6.

TRIPP, WALLACE. *The Tale of a Pig; A Caucasian Folktale.* Adapted and illustrated by author. New York: McGraw-Hill Book Co., 1968. Ages 5-9.

UCHIDA, YOSHIKO. *The Dancing Kettle and Other Japanese Folk Tales.* Illustrated by Richard C. Jones. New York: Harcourt, Brace & World, 1949. Grades 3-5.

UNTERMEYER, LOUIS. *The Firebringer and Other Great Stories; Fifty-five Legends that Live Forever.* Newly written. Illustrated by Mae Gerhard. Philadelphia: J. B. Lippincott Co., 1968. Grades 5-7.

WALKER, BARBARA. *Pigs and Pirates.* Illustrated by Harold Berson. New York: David White Co., 1969.

FOOD, SHELTER, TRANSPORTATION

ANDERSON, WILLIAM R. *First under the North Pole: The Voyage of the Nautilus.* Illustrated with photographs. New York: World Publishing Co., 1959. Grades 4-6.

BENDICK, JEANNE. *The First Book of Trains.* Illustrated by author. New York: Franklin Watts, 1955. Grades 3-5.

BENENSON, LAWRENCE A. *How a House Is Built.* Illustrated by Richard Lewis. New York: Criterion Books, 1965. Grades 4-6.

BERRY, ERICK. *Eating and Cooking around the World; Fingers before Forks.* Illustrated with photographs. New York: John Day Co., 1963. Grades 4-7.

BUEHR, WALTER. *Strange Craft.* Illustrated by author. New York: W. W. Norton & Co., 1962. Grades 4-6.

BURNS, WILLIAM A. *A World Full of Homes.* Illustrated by Paula Hutchinson. New York: McGraw-Hill Book Co., 1953. Grades 4-7.

COGGINS, JACK. *Nets Overboard: The Story of the Fishing Fleets.* Illustrated by author. New York: Dodd, Mead & Co., 1965. Grades 5-7.

COOKE, DAVID C. *Flights that Made History*. Illustrated. New York: G. P. Putnam's Sons, 1961. Grades 5-8.

COOMBS, CHARLES. *Lift Off: The Story of Rocket Power*. Illustrated by R. H. Foor. New York: William Morrow & Co., 1953. Grades 5-8.

CORBETT, SCOTT. *What Makes a Plane Fly?* Illustrated by Len Darwin. Boston: Little, Brown & Co., 1967. Grades 3-6.

COSGRAVE, JOHN O'HARA. *America Sails the Seas*. Illustrated by author. Boston: Houghton Mifflin Co., 1962. Grades 5-7.

DADIN, MICHAEL. *Submarines*. Photographs. Skokie, Ill.: Rand McNally & Co., 1963. Grades 7-9.

FRISCH, ROSE E. *Plants that Feed the World*. Illustrated by Denny McMains. Princeton, N.J.: D. Van Nostrand Co., 1966. Grades 4-6.

HENGESBAUGH, JAN R. *I Live in So Many Places*. Illustrated by Katherine Evans. Chicago: Children's Press, 1967.

HOLLING, HOLLING C. *Paddle-To-the-Sea*. Boston: Houghton Mifflin Co., 1941. Grades 4-6.

JACKSON, ROBERT B. *Road Race Round the World: New York to Paris*. Illustrated with photographs. New York: Henry Z. Walck, 1965. Grades 4-7.

LEE, LAURIE, AND LAMBERT, DAVID. *The Wonderful World of Transportation*. Garden City, N.Y.: Doubleday & Co., 1960. Grades 4 and up.

LEWELLEN, JOHN. *Helicopters: How They Work*. Illustrated by A. W. Revell. New York: Thomas Y. Crowell Co., 1955. Grades 4-6.

HOLIDAYS AND CELEBRATIONS

CAVANAH, FRANCES, AND PANNELL, LUCILLE, comps. *Holiday Roundup*. Illustrated by Elsie McCorkell. rev. ed. Philadelphia: Macrae Smith Co., 1968. Grades 4-6.

DOBLER, LAVINIA G. *National Holidays around the World*. Illustrated and designed by Vivian Browne. New York: Fleet Publishing Corp., 1968. Grades 4-9.

KEATS, EZRA JACK. *The Little Drummer Boy*. New York: Macmillan Co., 1968.

MENDOZA, GEORGE. *A Wart Snake in a Fig Tree*. New York: Dial Press, 1968.

MOORE, CLEMENT CLARKE. *A Visit from St. Nicholas*. Drawings by Paul Galdone. New York: McGraw-Hill Book Co., 1968. Grades Ps-3.

PATTERSON, LILLIE. *Christmas Feasts and Festivals*. Illustrated by Cliff Schule. Champaign, Ill.: Garrard Publishing Co., 1968. Grades 3-4.

PRESTON, EDNA MITCHELL. *One Dark Night*. Illustrated by Kurt Werth. New York: Viking Press, 1969. Grades Ps-K.

PIATTI, CELESTINE, AND VON JUCHEN, AUREL. *The Holy Night*. New York: Atheneum Publishers, 1968.

PURDY, SUSAN. *Festivals for You to Celebrate*. Illustrated. Philadelphia: J. B. Lippincott Co., 1969. Grades 4-8.

———. *Jewish Holidays; Facts, Activities and Crafts*. Illustrated by author. Philadelphia: J. B. Lippincott Co., 1969. Grades 4 and up.

REEVES, JAMES, comp. *The Christmas Book*. Illustrated by Raymond Briggs. New York: E. P. Dutton & Co., 1968. Grades 4-6.

WINTER, JEANETTE. *The Christmas Visitors*. New York: Pantheon Books, 1968.

INSECTS

ALLEN, GERTRUDE. *Everyday Insects*. Illustrated by author. Boston: Houghton Mifflin Co., 1963. Grades K-2.

BARANOWSKI, RICHARD. *Insects*. Illustrated with photographs. Racine, Wis.: Golden Press, Western Publishing Co., 1964. Grades 3-6.

BRONSON, WILFRED S. *The Grasshopper Book.* Illustrated by author. New York: Harcourt, Brace & World, 1943. Grades 4-7.

BROWN, VINSON. *How to Follow the Adventures of Insects.* Illustrated by Julia Iltis. Boston: Little, Brown & Co., 1968. Grades 6-10.

CLARKE, J. F. GATES. *Butterflies.* Illustrated by Andre Durenceau. Racine, Wis.: Golden Press, Western Publishing Co., 1963. Grades 4-7.

CONKLIN, GLADYS (PLEMON). *Lucky Ladybugs.* Drawings by Glen Rounds. New York: Holiday House, 1968. Grades K-3.

———. *When Insects Are Babies.* Pictures by Artur Marokvia. New York: Holiday House, 1969. Grades Ps-3.

EARLE, OLIVE L. *Praying Mantis.* Illustrated. New York: William Morrow & Co., 1969. Grades 2-4.

EPPLE, ANNE ORTH. *Ants.* Illustrated by Sally Kaicher. New York: Crowell Collier & Macmillan Co., 1969. Grades 1-4.

GREEN, IVAHM, AND SMITH, GEORGE A. *Hatch and Grow.* Photographs by George A. Smith. New York: Abelard-Schuman, 1968. Grades 5-7.

HOPE, ALICE L. *Monarch Butterflies.* Illustrated by Peter Burchard. New York: Thomas Y. Crowell Co., 1965. Grades 4-6.

HUNTINGTON, HARRIET *Let's Look at Insects.* Photographs by author. Drawings by J. Noel. Garden City, N.Y.: Doubleday & Co., 1969. Grades Ps-3.

HUTCHINS, CARLEEN. *Moon Moth.* Illustrated by Douglas Howland. New York: Coward-McCann, 1965. Grades 3-5.

HUTCHINS, ROSS E. *The Travels of Monarch X.* Illustrated by Jerome P. Connolly. Skokie, Ill.: Rand McNally & Co., 1966. Grades 2-5.

MITCHELL, ROBERT T., AND ZIM, HERBERT S. *Butterflies and Moths.* Illustrated by Andre Durenceau. Racine, Wis.: Golden Press, Western Publishing Co., 1964. Grades 4 and up.

PHILLIPS, MARY G. *Dragonflies and Damselflies.* Illustrated by Anne M. Jauss. New York: Thomas Y. Crowell, 1960. Grades 5-8.

RUSSELL, FRANKLIN. *The Honeybees.* Illustrated by Colette Portal. New York: Alfred A. Knopf, 1967. Grades 1-3.

SEARS, PAUL. *Firefly.* Illustrated by Glen Rounds. New York: Holiday House, 1956. Grades 4-6.

SELSAM, MILLICENT. *Questions and Answers about Ants.* Illustrated by Arabelle Wheatley. New York: Four Winds Press, Scholastic Book Services, 1967. Grades 2-5.

SHUTTLESWORTH, DOROTHY E. *All Kinds of Bees.* Illustrated by Su Zan Noguchi Swain. New York: Random House, 1967. Grades 3-5.

———. *The Story of Spiders.* Illustrated by Su Zan Noguchi Swain. Garden City, N.Y.: Doubleday & Co., 1959. Grades 5 and up.

STERLING, DOROTHY. *Caterpillars.* Illustrated by Winifred Lubell. Garden City, N.Y.: Doubleday & Co., 1961. Grades 3-6.

TIBBETS, ALBERT B. *The First Book of Bees.* Illustrated by Helene Carter. New York: Franklin Watts, 1952. Grades 5 and up.

VEVERS, HENRY GWYNNE. *Ants and Termites.* Illustrated by Colin Threadgall. New York: McGraw-Hill Book Co., 1966. Grades 3-6.

MAMMALS

BERGMAN SUCKSDORFF, ASTRID. *The Roe Deer.* Illustrated by author. Translated from Swedish by Alan Tapsell. New York: Harcourt, Brace & World, 1969. Grades 3-6.

BURGER, CARL. *All about Elephants.* Illustrated by author. New York: Random House, 1965. Grades 5-7.

DARLING, LOUIS. *Kangaroos and Other Animals with Pockets.* Illustrated by author. New York: William Morrow & Co., 1958. Grades 4-6.

——. *Seals and Walruses.* Illustrated by author. New York: William Morrow & Co., 1955. Grades 4-6.

DUGDALE, VERA. *Album of North American Animals.* Illustrated by Clark Bronson. Skokie, Ill.: Rand McNally & Co., 1966. Grades 5-7.

GOUDEY, ALICE E. *Here Come the Squirrels!* Illustrated by Garry Mackenzie. New York: Charles Scribner's Sons, 1962. Grades 3-6.

——. *Here Come the Lions!* Illustrated by Garry Mackenzie. New York: Charles Scribner's Sons, 1956. Grades 3-6.

——. *Here Come the Cottontails!* Illustrated by Garry Mackenzie. New York: Charles Scribner's Sons, 1965. Grades 3-6.

HESS, LILO. *Foxes in the Woodshed.* Photographs. New York: Charles Scribner's Sons, 1966. Grades 2-3.

——. *The Curious Raccoons.* Photographs. New York: Charles Scribner's Sons, 1968. Grades 2-3.

HUDSON, ROBERT G. *Nature's Nursery; Baby Mammals.* Illustrated. New York: John Day Co., 1969. Grades 4-7.

LAUBER, PATRICIA. *The Friendly Dolphins.* Illustrated by Jean Simpson. New York: Random House, 1963. Grades 3-4.

——. *Bats: Wings in the Night.* New York: Random House, 1968. Grades 4-6.

LIERS, EMIL E. *An Otter's Story.* Illustrated by Tony Palazzo. New York: Viking Press, 1953. Grades 4-7.

RIPPER, CHARLES L. *The Weasel Family.* Illustrated by author. New York: William Morrow & Co., 1959. Grades 4-6.

RUSSELL, FRANKLIN. *The Frightened Hare.* Illustrated by Fredric Sweney. New York: Holt, Rinehart & Winston, 1965. Grades 3-5.

SCHALLER, GEORGE B., AND SELSAM, MILLICENT E. *The Tiger; It's Life in the Wild.* New York: Harper & Row, Publishers, 1969. Grades 4-8.

SCHWARTZ, ELIZABETH AND CHARLES. *Cottontail Rabbit.* Illustrated. New York: Holiday House, 1957. Grades 4-6.

WILLIAMSON, MARGARET. *The First Book of Mammals.* New York: Franklin Watts, 1957. Grades 4-7.

ZIM, HERBERT S. *Monkeys.* Illustrated. New York: William Morrow & Co., 1955. Grades 4-7.

——. *The Big Cats.* Illustrated. New York: William Morrow & Co., 1955. Grades 4-7.

——. *The Great Whales.* Illustrated. New York: William Morrow & Co., 1951. Grades 4-7.

MAPS

DUVOISIN, ROGER A. *They Put Out to Sea: The Story of the Map.* Illustrated by author. New York: Alfred A. Knopf, 1944. Grades 5-7.

EPSTEIN, SAM AND BERYL. *The First Book of Maps and Globes.* New York: Franklin Watts, 1959. Grades 4 and up.

HIRSCH, S. CARL. *The Globe for the Space Age.* Illustrated by Burt Silverman. New York: Viking Press, 1963. Grades 5-8.

MARSH, SUSAN. *All about Maps and Map Making.* Illustrated with maps and photographs. New York: Random House, 1963. Grades 5-7.

QUINN, VERNON. *Picture Map Geography of the United States.* Philadelphia: J. B. Lippincott Co., 1959. Grades 4-8.

RINKOFF, BARBARA. *A Map Is a Picture.* Illustrated by Robert Galster. New York: Thomas Y. Crowell Co., 1965. Grades K-2.

TANNENBAUM, BEULAH, AND STILLMAN, MYRA. *Understanding Maps; Charting the Land, Sea and Sky.* rev. ed. Illustrated by Adolph E. Brotman and with photographs. New York: McGraw-Hill Book Co., 1969. Grades 6-9.

MATHEMATICS

ABISCH, ROZ. *Do You Know What Time It Is?* Illustrated by Boche Kaplan. Englewood Cliffs, N.J.: Prentice-Hall, 1968. Grades Ps-3.

ADLER, IRVING. *Time In Your Life.* Illustrated by Ruth Adler. rev. ed. New York: John Day Co., 1969. Grades 5-8.

ADLER, IRVING AND RUTH. *Numerals, New Dresses for Old Numbers.* New York: John Day Co., 1964. Grades 5-8.

———. *Numbers Old and New.* Illustrated by Peggy Adler. New York: John Day Co., 1960. Grades 5-7.

ADLER, IRVING AND RUTH. *Sets and Numbers for the Very Young.* Illustrated by Peggy Adler. New York: John Day Co., 1969. Grades Ps-1.

———. *The Calendar.* New York: John Day Co., 1967. Grades 4-6.

ALAIN, PSEUD. (EMILE CHARTIER). *One, Two, Three, Going to Sea.* New York: William R. Scott, 1964.

ALLEN, ROBERT. *Count with Me.* Illustrated by Edith Witt. New York: Platt & Munk Co., 1969. Grades Ps-3.

ANDREWS, FRANK EMERSON. *Numbers Please.* Illustrated by Aldren A. Watson. Boston: Little, Brown & Co., 1961. Grades 5-8.

ASIMOV, ISAAC. *Quick and Easy Math.* Boston: Houghton-Mifflin Co., 1964.

BARR, CATHRINE. *99 Ducks Plus 1.* Illustrated by author. New York: Henry Z. Walck, 1969. Grades Ps-2.

BARR, DONALD. *Arithmetic for Billy Goats.* Illustrated by Don Madden. New York: Harcourt, Brace & World, 1966. Grades 4-6.

BEHN, HARRY. *All Kinds of Time.* Illustrated by author. New York: Harcourt, Brace & World, 1950. Grades 1-3.

BENDICK, JEANNE. *Shapes.* Illustrated by author. New York: Franklin Watts, n.d. Grades 2-4.

———. *Space and Time.* Illustrated by author. New York: Franklin Watts, 1968. Grades 2-4.

BENDICK, JEANNE. *The First Book of Time.* Illustrated by author. New York: Franklin Watts, 1963. Grades 4-6.

BENDICK, JEANNE, AND LEVIN, MARCIA. *Take a Number.* New York: McGraw-Hill Book Co., 1961. Grades 4-5.

———. *Take a Number; New Ideas and Imagination = More Fun.* New York: Whittlesey House, McGraw-Hill Book Co., 1961. Grades 4-8.

———. *Take Shapes, Lines, and Letters.* Pictures by Jeanne Bendick. New York: Whittlesey House, McGraw-Hill Book Co., 1962. Grades 5 and up.

BERG, JEAN. *Bigger than an Elephant.* Illustrated by author. New York: Crown Publishers, 1968. Grades Ps-1.

BORLAND, KATHRYN KILBY, AND SPEICHER, HELEN ROSS. *Clocks, From Shadow to Atom.* Illustrated by Robert Addison. Chicago: Follett Publishing Co., 1969. Grades 3-5.

CARLE, ERIC. *1, 2, 3 to the Zoo.* Colored illustrations. New York: World Publishing Co., 1968. Grades Ps-1.

CARONA, PHILIP B. *Things That Measure.* Illustrated by John Kaufmann. Englewood Cliffs, N.J.: Prentice-Hall, 1962. Grades 3-5.

CLARK, FRANK. *Speed Math.* New York: Franklin Watts, 1968. Grades 4 and up.

CREWS, DONALD. *Ten Black Dots.* New York: Charles Scribner's Sons, 1968. Grades Ps-3.

DIGGINS, JULIA. *String, Straightedge and Shadow, The Story of Geometry.* New York: Viking Press, 1965.

DILSON, JESSE. *The Abacus: A Pocket Computer.* Drawings by Angela Pozzi. New York: St. Martin's Press, 1968. Grades 5-8.

DUVOISIN, ROGER. *Two Lonely Ducks.* New York: Alfred A. Knopf, 1955.

EMBERLEY, BARBARA. *One Wide River to Cross.* Illustrated by Ed Emberley. Englewood Cliffs, N.J.: Prentice-Hall, 1966. Grades K-3.

FREEMAN, MAE. *Finding Out about Shapes.* Illustrated by Bill Morrison. New York: McGraw-Hill Book Co., 1969. Grades 2-4.

GARDNER, MARTIN. *Archimedes, Mathematician and Inventor.* Illustrated by Leonard Everett Fisher. New York: Macmillan Co., 1965. Grades 3-5.

GRAMET, CHARLES. *Highways across Waterways; Ferries, Bridges and Tunnels.* New York: Abelard-Schuman, 1967.

HALEY, GAIL. *One, Two, Buckle My Shoe; A Book of Counting Rhymes.* Illustrated. Garden City, N.Y.: Doubleday & Co., 1964. Grades Ps-3.

HIRSCH, S. CARL. *This Is Automation.* Illustrated by Anthony Ravielli. New York: Viking Press, 1964. Grades 5-7.

JONAS, ARTHUR. *More New Ways in Math.* Illustrated by Aliki. Englewood Cliffs, N.J.: Prentice-Hall, 1964. Grades 4-6.

———. *New Ways in Math.* Illustrated by Aliki. Englewood Cliffs, N.J.: Prentice-Hall, 1962. Grades 3-6.

JUPO, FRANK. *A Day around the World.* New York: Abelard-Schuman, 1968. Grades K-3.

KENYON, RAYMOND G. *I Can Learn about Calculators and Computers.* Drawings by author. New York: Harper & Row, Publishers, 1961. Grades 6-9.

KOHN, BERNICE. *Everything Has a Shape.* Illustrated by Aliki. Englewood Cliffs, N.J.: Prentice-Hall, 1964.

———. *Everything Has a Size.* Englewood Cliffs, N.J.: Prentice-Hall, 1965.

KRUSS, JAMES. *3 x 3 Three by Three.* Translated by Geoffrey Strachan. Illustrated by Johanna Rubin. New York: Macmillan Co., 1965. Grades Ps-K.

LAUBER, PATRICIA. *The Story of Numbers.* Illustrated by Mircea Vasiliu. New York: Random House, 1961. Grades 3-5.

McLEOD, EMILIE WARREN. *One Snail and Me.* Illustrated by Walter Lorraine. Boston: Little, Brown & Co., 1961. Grades Ps-1.

MOORE, WILLIAM. *How Fast? How Far? How Much?* Illustrated. New York: G. P. Putnam's Sons, 1966. Grades 4-7.

NAVARRA, JOHN GABRIEL. *Clocks, Calendars, and Carrousels.* Illustrated by Al Nagy. Garden City, N.Y.: Doubleday & Co., 1967. Grades 4-6.

O'NEILL, MARY (LE DUC). *Take a Number.* Illustrated by Al Nagy. Garden City, N.Y.: Doubleday & Co., 1968. Grades 1-4.

PLOTZ, HELEN. *Imagination's Other Place.* Illustrated by Clare Leighton. New York: Thomas Y. Crowell Co., 1955. Grades 7 and up.

RAZZELL, ARTHUR G., AND WATTS, K. G. O. *A Question of Accuracy.* Exploring Mathematics Series. Illustrated by Ellen Raskin. Garden City, N.Y.: Doubleday & Co., 1969. Grades Ps-6.

———. *Probability: The Science of Chance.* Illustrated by Ellen Raskin. Garden City, N.Y.: Doubleday & Co., 1967. Grades 5-8.

RECK, ALMA KEHOE. *Clocks Tell the Time.* Illustrated by Janina Domanska. New York: Charles Scribner's Sons, 1963. Grades 4-6..

REIT, SEYMOUR. *Round Things Everywhere.* Full color photographs by Carol Basen. New York: McGraw Hill Book Co., 1969. Grades 4-8. My World Series.

RUSSELL, SOLVEIG. *Lines and Shapes: A First Look at Geometry.* Illustrated by Arnold Spilka. New York: Henry Z. Walck, 1965. Grades 1-4.

ROTHMAN, JOEL, AND TREMAIN, RUTHVEN. *Secrets with Ciphers and Codes.* Illustrated. New York: Macmillan Co., 1969. Grades 3 and up.

SPINK, MICHAEL. *The 1, 2, 3 Frieze.* New York: E. P. Dutton & Co., 1969.

TANNENBAUM, BEULAH, AND STILLMAN, MYRA. *Understanding Time: The Science of Clocks and Calendars.* Illustrated by William D. Hayes. New York: McGraw-Hill Book Co., 1958. Grades 5-8.

TUDOR, TASHA. *1 Is One.* New York: Henry Z. Walck, 1956.

WHITNEY, DAVID C. *The Easy Book of Multiplication.* Illustrated by Sheila Granda. New York: Franklin Watts, 1969. Grades 3-5.

ZOLOTOW, CHARLOTTE. *One Step, Two . . .* Illustrated by Roger Duvoisin. New York: Lathrop, Lee & Shepard Co., 1955.

MEN AND WORK

AGLE, NAN H., AND WILSON, ELLEN. *Three Boys and a Lighthouse.* Illustrated by Martin Honigman. New York: Charles Scribner's Sons, 1951. Grades 1-3.

ALTERMAN, HYMAN. *Counting People: The Census in History.* Charts and graphs. New York: Harcourt, Brace & World, 1969., Grades 7 and up.

ANDERSON, JOHN LONZO. *Bag of Smoke; The Story of Man's First Reach for Space,* by Lonzo Anderson. Illustrated by Adrienne Adams. New York: Alfred A. Knopf, 1968. Grades 4-6.

ASIMOV, ISAAC. *Great Ideas of Science.* Illustrated by Lee Ames. Boston: Houghton Mifflin Co., 1969. Grades 7 and up.

BATE, NORMAN. *Who Built the Bridge?* Illustrated. New York: Charles Scribner's Sons, 1954. Grades K-3.

BUEHR, WALTER. *Rubber: Natural and Synthetic.* Illustrated by author. New York: William Morrow & Co., 1964. Grades 4-6.

———. *Treasure: The Story of Money and Its Safeguarding.* Illustrated by author. New York: G. P. Putnam's Sons, 1955. Grades 4-6.

BURT, OLIVE W. *The Story of American Railroads and How They Helped Build a Nation.* Illustrated. New York: John Day Co., 1969. Grades 5-9.

CALVERT, JAMES. *A Promise to Our Country: "I Pledge Allegiance . . ."* Illustrated by James Daugherty. New York: McGraw-Hill Book Co., 1961. Grades 3-6.

COLBY, CARROLL B. *The National Guard; Purpose, Training and Equipment.* Illustrated. New York: Coward-McCann, 1968. Grades 5 and up.

COMPTON, GRANT. *What Does a Coast Guardsman Do?* Illustrated, coats of arms. New York: Dodd, Mead & Co., 1968. Grades 4-7.

COOKE, DAVID C. *How Paper Is Made.* Illustrated with photographs. New York: Dodd, Mead & Co., 1959. Grades 4-6.

COOMBS, CHARLES. *Cleared for Takeoff, Behind the Scenes at an Airport.* Illustrated with photographs. New York: William Morrow & Co., 1969. Grades 7 and up.

DESMOND, ALICE C. *Your Flag and Mine.* New York: Macmillan Co., 1960. Grades 5-7.

DOHERTY, CHARLES HUGH. *Tunnels.* Illustrated by Michael Baker. Des Moines: Meredith Corp., 1968. Grades 6-9.

EPSTEIN, EDNA. *The First Book of the United Nations.* rev. ed. New York: Franklin Watts, 1966. Grades 7-10.

EPSTEIN, SAM AND BERYL. *The First Book of Glass.* Illustrated by Bette J. Davis. New York: Franklin Watts, 1955. Grades 3-5.

FEHRENBACH, T. R. *The United Nations in War and Peace.* Illustrated, maps. New York: Random House, 1968. Grades 6-9.

FENTEN, D. X. *Aviation Careers, Jobs in the Air and on the Ground.* Photographs. Philadelphia: J. B. Lippincott Co., 1969. Grades 7 and up.

FISHER, LEONARD EVERETT. *The Doctors.* Illustrated by author. New York: Franklin Watts, 1968. Grades 4-7.

GLASSNER, SHERWIN S., AND GROSSMAN, EDWARD N. *How the American Economic System Functions.* Illustrated by Michael A. Norman. Westchester, Ill.: Benefic Press, 1968. Grades 5-7.

GREENE, CARLA. *I Want to Be a Dentist.* Illustrated. Chicago: Children's Press, 1960. Grades 1-3.

———. *I Want to Be a Musician.* Chicago: Children's Press. 1962. Grades 1-3.

———. *Soldiers and Sailors: What Do They Do?* Illustrated by Leonard Kessler. New York: Harper & Row, Publishers, 1963. Grades 1-2.

GREY, ELIZABETH. *The Story of Journalism.* Illustrated with photographs. Boston: Houghton Mifflin Co., 1969. Grades 7 and up.

HAMMOND, WINIFRED G. *Cotton from Farm to Market.* Illustrated, maps. New York: Coward-McCann, 1968. Grades 3-6.

HUNTINGTON, HARRIET E. *Cargoes.* Illustrated with photographs. Garden City, N.Y.: Doubleday & Co., 1964. Grades 4-7.

IPCAR, DAHLOV. *Ten Big Farms.* Illustrated by author. New York: Alfred A. Knopf, 1958. Grades K-4.

JAMES, LEONARD FRANK. *Following the Frontier; American Transportation in the Nineteenth Century.* Illustrated by Raymond Houlihan. New York: Harcourt, Brace & World, 1968. Grades 5-7.

JOHNSON, GERALD W. *The Cabinet.* Illustrated by Leonard E. Fisher. New York: William Morrow & Co., 1966. Grades 5-7.

———. *The Congress.* Illustrated by Leonard E. Fisher. New York: William Morrow & Co., 1963. Grades 5-7.

———. *The Presidency.* Illustrated by Leonard E. Fisher. New York: William Morrow & Co., 1962. Grades 5-7.

———. *The Supreme Court.* Illustrated by Leonard E. Fisher. New York: William Morrow & Co., 1962. Grades 5-7.

KAHN, ELY JACQUES. *A Building Goes Up.* Illustrated by Cal Sacks. New York: Simon & Schuster, 1969. Grades 4-6.

LENT, HENRY BOLLES. *Agriculture U.S.A.: America's Most Basic Industry.* Illustrated. New York: E. P. Dutton & Co., 1968. Grades 5-8.

LINDOP, EDMUND. *The First Book of Electrons.* Illustrated by Gustave E. Nebel. New York: Franklin Watts, 1968. Grades 4-6.

MIERS, EARL S. *The Capitol and Our Lawmakers.* Illustrated with photographs. New York: Grosset & Dunlap, 1965. Grades 5-7.

———. *The White House and the Presidency.* Illustrated with photographs. New York: Grosset & Dunlap, 1965. Grades 5-7.

MINER, IRENE. *The True Book of Policemen and Firemen.* Illustrated by Mary Salem. Chicago: Children's Press, 1954. Grades 1-3.

RAPPAPORT, EVA. *Banner Forward.* The Pictorial Biography of a Guide Dog. Illustrated with photographs. New York: E. P. Dutton & Co., 1969. Grades 5 and up.

RIDLEY, ANTHONY. *An Illustrated History of Transportation.* New York: John Day Co., 1969. Grades 7 and up.

RAY, E. ROY. *What Does an Airplane Crew Do?* Photographs by Martin Harris. New York: Dodd, Mead & Co., 1968. Grades 4-7.

RUBICAM, HARRY C. *Men at Work on the West Coast.* Illustrated with photographs. New York: G. P. Putnam's Sons, 1959. Grades 4-6.

———. *Men at Work in the Great Lakes States.* Illustrated with photographs. New York: G. P. Putnam's Sons, 1958. Grades 4-6.

———. *Men at Work in New England.* rev. ed. Illustrated with photographs. New York: G. P. Putnam's Sons, 1967. Grades 4-6.

SCHNEIDER, HERMAN AND NINA. *Let's Look under the City.* Illustrated by Bill Ballantine. New York: William R. Scott, 1954. Grades 3-6.

SHAY, ARTHUR. *What Happens When You Put Money in the Bank.* Photographs. Chicago: Reilly & Lee Co., 1967. Grades 1-3.

———. *What Happens at a Television Station.* Photographs. Chicago: Reilly & Lee Co., n.d. Grades 1-3.

———. *What Happens When You Mail a Letter.* Photographs. Chicago: Reilly & Lee Co., Grades 1-3.

——. *What Happens When You Make a Telephone Call.* Photographs. Chicago: Reilly & Lee Co., n.d. Grades 1-3.
——. *What Happens in a Car Factory.* Photographs. Chicago: Reilly & Lee Co., n.d. Grades 1-3.
——. *What Happens When You Go to the Hospital.* Photographs. Chicago: Reilly & Lee Co., n.d. Grades 1-3.
SPEISPER, JEAN. *UNICEF and the World.* Illustrated with photographs. New York: John Day Co., 1965. Grades 4-6.
TORBERT, FLOYD J. *Policemen the World Over.* Illustrated by author. New York: Hastings House, 1965. Grades 4-6.
WELLS, ROBERT. *What Does a Test Pilot Do?* Photographs and charts. New York: Dodd, Mead & Co., 1969. Grades 3-7.

OCEANOGRAPHY

BERGAUST, ERICK, AND FOSS, WILLIAM O. *Oceanographers in Action.* New York: G. P. Putnam's Sons, 1968. Grades 5-8.
BRIGGS, PETER. *Men in the Sea.* New York: Simon & Schuster, Inc., 1968. Grades 7-9.
——. *The Great Global Rift.* Illustrated by David Noyes. New York: Weybright & Talley, 1969. Grades 5-8.
COX, DONALD WILLIAM. *Explorers of the Deep; Pioneers of Oceanography.* Illustrater by Jack Woodson. Maplewood, N.J.: Hammand and Company, 1968. Grades 5-9.
SHANNON, TERRY, AND PAYZANT, CHARLES. *The Sea Searchers; Men and Machines at the Bottom of the Sea.* Los Angeles: Golden Gate Junior Books, 1968. Grades 5-9.
WATERS, JOHN F. *What Does on Oceanographer Do?* Illustrated with photographs. New York: Dodd, Mead & Co., Inc., 1969. Grades 3-5.

PLANTS, NATURE & WEATHER

ARNOV, BORIS. *Homes Beneath the Sea; An Introduction to Ocean Ecology.* Boston: Little, Brown and Co., 1969. Grades 6-9.
BAKER, JEFFERY J. W. *Patterns of Nature.* Photographs by Jaroslav Salek. Garden City, N.Y.: Doubleday & Company, Inc., 1967. Grades K-4.
——. *The Vital Process, Photosynthesis.* Illustrated by Particia Collins. Garden City, N.Y.: Doubleday & Company, Inc., 1969. Grades K-5.
BELL, THELMA. *Snow.* Illustrated by Corydon Bell. New York: The Viking Press, Inc., 1954. Grades 4-6.
BENDICK, JEANNE. *The Wind.* Illustrated by author. Skokie, Ill.: Rand McNally & Co., 1964. Grades 3-4.
BENTLEY, LINNA. *Plants That Eat Animals.* Illustrated by Colin Threadgall. New York: McGraw-Hill Book Co., Inc., 1968. Grades 4-6.
BRANDHORST, CARL T., AND SYLVESTER, ROBERT. *The Tale of Whitefoot.* Illustrated by Grambs Miller. New York: Simon & Schuster, Inc., 1968. Grades 3-5.
BUCK, MARGARET, WARING. *Along the Seashore.* Illustrated by the author. Nashville: Abingdon Press, 1964. Grades 3-7.
CARRICK, CAROL, AND CARRICK, DONALD. *Swamp Spring.* New York: The Macmillan Co., 1969. Grades K-3.
COLE, WILLIAM, Compiler. *A Book of Nature Poems.* Illustrated by Robert Andrew Parker. New York: The Viking Press, Inc., 1968. Grades 5-9.

COOPER, ELIZABETH K. *Science in Your Own Backyard.* New York: Harcourt, Brace & World, Inc., 1958. Grades 5-8.

DUDLEY, RUTH H. *Partners in Nature.* Illustrated by Eva Cellini. New York: F. & W., 1965. Grades 5-7.

FACKLAM, MARGERY. *Behind These Doors: Science Museum Makers.* Skokie, Ill.: Rand McNally & Co., 1968. Grades 6-9.

FENTON, CARROLL L., AND KITCHEN, HERMINIE B. *Plants That Feed Us.* Illustrated by Carroll L. Fenton. New York: The John Day Co., 1956. Grades 4-7.

———, AND FENTON, MILDRED A. *Our Changing Weather.* Garden City, N.Y.: Doubleday & Co., Inc., 1954. Grades 5-8.

FOX, CHARLES PHILIP. *When Winter Comes.* Illustrated with photographs. Chicago: Reilly & Lee Co., 1962. Grades K-1.

GOLDIN, AUGUSTA R. *The Sunlit Sea.* Illustrated by Paul Galdone. New York: Thomas Y. Crowell Co., 1968. Grades 2-3.

GOUDEY, ALICE E. *The Day We Saw the Sun Come Up.* Illustrated by Adrienne Adams. New York: Charles Scribner's Sons, 1961. Grades PreK-1.

IRVING, ROBERT. *Hurricanes and Twisters.* Illustrated by Ruth Adler and with photographs. New York: Alfred A. Knopf, Inc., 1955. Grades 4-7.

KANE, HENRY BUGBEE. *Four Seasons in the Woods.* Illustrated by author. New York: Alfred A. Knopf, Inc., 1968. Grades 2-4.

———. *The Tale of a Meadow.* Illustrated by author. New York: Alfred A. Knopf, Inc., 1959. Grades 4-7.

———. *The Tale of a Wood.* Illustrated by author. New York: Alfred A. Knopf, Inc., 1962. Grades 4-7.

KAVALER, LUCY. *Dangerous Air.* Illustrated by Carl Smith. New York: The John Day Co., Inc., 1967. Grades 6-9.

KLEIN, RICHARD M., AND KLEIN, DEANA T. *Discovering Plants: A Nature and Science Book of Experiments.* New York: Natural History Press, 1969. Grades 4-7.

KOHN, BERNICE. *Ferns: Plants Without Flowers.* Illustrated by Penelope Naylor. New York, Hawthorn Books, Inc., 1968. Grades 4-6.

LEHR, PAUL E. *Storms: Their Origins and Effects, Forecasting and Weather Lore.* Illustrated by Harry McNaught and Nino Carbe. New York: Western Publishing Co., 1966. Grades 4-6.

LERNER, SHARON. *I Found a Leaf.* Illustrated by author. Minneapolis: Lerner Publications Co., 1964. Grades K-2.

LUBELL, WINIFRED AND CECIL. *Green Is for Growing.* Illustrated by Winifred Lubell. Skokie, Ill.: Rand McNally & Co., 1964. Grades 2-4.

NAVARRA, JOHN GABRIEL. *Wide World Weather.* Garden City, N.Y.: Doubleday & Company, Inc., 1968. Grades 6-8.

PARKER, BERTHA MORRIS. *The New Golden Treasury of Natural History.* Racine, Wis.: Golden Press, Western Publishing Co., 1968. Grades 3-7.

PINE, TILLIE S., AND LEVINE, JOSEPH. *Trees and How We Use Them.* Illustrated by Bernice Myers. New York: McGraw-Hill Book Co., Inc., 1969. Grades 2-6.

SCHIMA, MARILYN, AND BOLIAN, POLLY. *Something Grows.* Three-color illustrations by Polly Bolian. Englewood Cliffs, N.J.: Prentice-Hall, Inc., 1969. Grades PreK-3.

SILVERSTEIN, ALVIN, AND SILVERSTEIN, VIRGINIA B. *Unusual Partners; Symbiosis in the Living World.* Illustrated by Mel Hunter. New York: McGraw-Hill Book Co., 1968. Grades 4-6.

SIMON, SEYMOUR. *Weather and Climate.* Illustrated by John Polgreen. New York: Random House, Inc., 1969. Grades 5-7.

SLOAN, TAY. *Wonder of the Pacific Shore.* Photographs by author. Drawings by Lura Karlsson. Additional illustrations by Robert Borja. Chicago: Children's Press, 1968. Grades 4-6.

SLOTE, ALFRED. *Air in Fact and Fancy.* Illustrations by Dan Dickas. Cleveland: The World Publishing Co., 1968. Grades 4-7.

STONE, A. HARRIS, AND LESKOWITZ, IRVING. *Plants Are Like That*. Illustrated by Peter P. Plasencia. Englewood Cliffs, N.J.: Prentice-Hall, Inc., 1968. Grades 4-7.

WEBSTER, DAVID. *Snow Stumpers*. New York: Natural History Press, 1968. Grades PreK-1.

WEISGARD, LEONARD. *The First Farmers in the New Stone Age*. Illustrated by author. New York: Coward-McCann, 1966. Grades 4-7.

WINCHESTER, JAMES H. *Hurricanes, Storms, Tornadoes*. New York: G. P. Putnam's Sons, 1968. Grades 5-9.

THE BODY AND SEX EDUCATION

ELGIN, KATHLEEN. *The Human Body: The Heart*. Illustrated by author. New York: Franklin Watts, Inc., 1968. Grades 2-4.

ETS, MARIE HALL. *The Story of a Baby*. Illustrated by author. New York: The Viking Press, Inc., 1969. Grades 3-7.

GOLDIN, AUGUSTA. *Straight Hair, Curly Hair*. Illustrated by Ed Emberley. New York: Crowell Collier & Macmillan Co., 1966. Grades K-2.

GORDON, SOL. *Facts About Sex*. New York: The John Day Co., Inc., 1969. All grades.

GRUENBERG, SIDONIE MATSNER. *The Wonderful Story of How You Were Born*. Illustrated by Symeon Shimin. Revised Edition. Garden City, N.Y.: Doubleday & Co., Inc., 1970. Grades 3-5.

HOFSTEIN, SADIE. *The Human Story; Facts on Birth, Growth and Reproduction*. New York: Lothrop, Lee & Shepard Co., 1968. All grades.

LIBERTY, GENE. *The First Book of the Human Senses*. Illustrated by Robert Todd. New York: Franklin Watts, 1961. Grades 4-7.

McNEEL, JOHN P. *The Brain of Man*. Illustrated by Lee Ames. New York: G. P. Putnam's Sons, 1968. Grades 6-8.

NAVARRA, JOHN G., WEISBERG, JOSEPH S., AND MELE, FRANK M. *From Generation to Generation: The Story of Reproduction*. New York: Natural History Press, 1969. All grades.

SCHUMAN, BENJAMIN N. *The Human Eye*. Drawings by Michael K. Meyers. New York: Atheneum Publishers, 1968. Grades 3-6.

SHOWERS, PAUL, AND SHOWERS, KAY SPERRY. *Before You Were a Baby*. Illustrated by Ingrid Fetz. New York: Thomas Y. Crowell Co., 1968. All grades.

———. *How You Talk*. Illustrated by Robert Galster. New York: Thomas Y. Crowell Company, 1966. Grades K-2.

———. *Your Skin and Mine*. Illustrated by Paul Galdone. New York: Thomas Y. Crowell Co., 1965. Grades 1-3.

SILVERSTEIN, ALVIN, AND SILVERSTEIN, VIRGINIA B. *Cells: Building Blocks of Life*. Illustrated by George Bakacs. Englewood Cliffs, N.J.: Prentice-Hall, Inc., 1969. Grades 3-7.

WEART, EDITH. *The Story of Your Brain and Nerves*. Illustrated by Alan Tompkins. New York: Coward-McCannu, 1961. Grades 5-7.

ZIM, HERBERT S. *Bones*. Illustrated by Rene Martin. New York: William Morrow & Co., 1969. Grades 3-7.

THE UNITED STATES

ARBITAL, SAMUEL L. *Cities and Metropolitan Areas*. Mankato, Minn.: Creative Educational Society, 1967. Grades 5-9.

BAILEY, BERNADINE. *The United States Books*. Illustrated by Kurt Wiese. Chicago: Albert Whitman and Co. Grades 3-5.

BAUER, HELEN. *Hawaii, The Aloha State*. Garden City, N.Y.: Doubleday and Co., Inc., 1960. Grades 4-7.

BUEHR, WALTER. *Salt, Sugar, and Spice*. New York: William Morrow & Co., 1969. Grades 4-6.

BUFF, MARY (MARSH), AND BUFF, CONRAD. *The Colorado: River of Mystery*. Los Angeles: Ward Ritchie Press, 1968. Grades 4-6.

CARPENTER, ALLAN. *Florida: From Its Glorious Past to the Present*. Chicago: Children's Press, 1965. Grades 4-6.

———. *New Jersey: From Its Glorious Past to the Present*. Chicago: Children's Press, 1965. Grades 4-6.

———. *Oregon: From Its Glorious Past to the Present*. Chicago: Children's Press, 1965. Grades 4-6.

CHENEY, T. A. *Land of the Hibernating Rivers; Life in the Arctic*. New York: Harcourt, Brace & World, Inc., 1968. Grades 6-8.

DAY, A. GOVE. *Hawaii: Fiftieth Star*. Illustrated with photographs. Des Moines: Meredith Corporation, 1969. Grades 5-8.

EPSTEIN, SAM AND BERYL. *The First Book of Washington, D. C., The Nation's Capital*. New York: Franklin Watts, 1961. Grades 4-6.

HOLLAND, JOHN, Editor. *The Way It Is*. Foreword by J. Anthony Lukas. New York: Harcourt, Brace & World, Inc., 1969. Grades 5 and up.

IPCAR, DAHLOV. *Lobsterman*. Illustrated by author. New York: Alfred A. Knopf, Inc., 1962. Grades 1-3.

LINDQUIST, WILLIS. *Alaska: The Forty-Ninth State*. Illustrated by P. A. Hutchinson. New York: McGraw-Hill Book Co., 1959. Grades 4-6.

LARRICK, NANCY, Compiler. *On City Streets; An Anthology of Poetry*. Illustrated with photographs by David Sagarin. Philadelphia: J. B. Lippincott Co., 1968. Grades 4-9.

McCLOSKEY, ROBERT. *One Morning in Maine*. Illustrated by author. New York: Viking Press, 1952. Grades 1-3.

McNEER, MAY. *The Story of the Southwest*. Illustrated by C. H. DeWitt. Evanston, Ill.: Harper and Row, 1948. Grades 4-7.

MILES, MISKA. *Mississippi Possum*. Illustrated by John Schenherr. Boston: Little, Brown and Co., 1965. Grades 1-3.

MUNZER, MARTHA E. *Pockets of Hope; Studies of Land and People*. Maps by John Bierhorst. New York: Alfred A. Knopf, Inc., 1967. Grades 7-9.

PEDERSEN, ELSA. *Alaska*. Consultant: Roscoe E. Bell. New York: Coward-McCann, 1969. Grades 6-9.

POLITI, LEOS. *Song of the Swallows*. Illustrated by author. New York: Charles Scribner's Sons, 1949. Grades K-3.

RAWLINGS, MARJORIE K. *The Secret River*. Illustrated by Leonard Weisgard. New York: Charles Scribner's Sons, 1955. Grades 2-5.

SASEK, M. *This is Paris*. New York: The Macmillan Company, 1959. Grades 4 and up.

———. *This is Washington, D. C.* Illustrated by author. New York: The Macmillan Company, 1970. Grades 4 and up.

SCHERE, MONROE. *Your Changing City*. Illustrated by Erwin Schachner. Englewood Cliffs, N.J.: Prentice-Hall, Inc., 1969. Grades 3-7.

SCHWARTZ, ALVIN. *Old Cities and New Towns; The Changing Face of the Nation*. New York: E. P. Dutton and Co., 1968. Grades 6-8.

SELVEN, DAVID F. *The Other San Francisco*. Drawings and maps by Joseph Papin. New York: Seabury Press, 1969. Grades 6 and up.

SILVERBERG, ROBERT. *Ghost Towns of the American West*. Illustrated by Lorence Bjorklund. New York: Thomas Y. Crowell Co., 1968. Grades 3-6.

VOGEL, RAY. *The Other City.* With photographs and commentary by William Boyd, James Freeman, Alfonso Garcia and Ronald McCoy. New York: David White Co., 1969. Grades 5 and up.

U.S. HISTORY & INDIANS

BALDWIN, GORDON C. *How the Indians Really Lived.* New York: G. P. Putnam's Sons, 1967. Grades 5-8.

BAUER, HELEN. *California Indian Days.* Line drawings by Don Freeman. Revised edition. Garden City, N.Y.: Doubleday & Co., Inc., 1968. Grades 4-7.

BAYLOR, BYRD. *Before You Came This Way.* Illustrated by Tom Bahti. New York: E. P. Dutton and Co., 1969. All grades.

BREWSTER, BENJAMIN. *The First Book of Indians.* New York: Franklin Watts, 1950. Grades 4-6.

CAMPBELL, ELIZABETH ANDERSON. *The Carving on the Tree.* Illustrated by William Bock. Boston: Little, Brown and Co., 1968. Grades 3-5.

CAVANAH, FRANCES. *Our Country's Story.* Illustrated by Julia Keats. Skokie, Ill.: Rand McNally & Co., 1962. Grades 2-4.

CAVANAH, FRANCES, AND CRANDALL, ELIZABETH L. *Freedom Encyclopedia: American Liberties in the Making.* Illustrated by Lorence F. Bjorklund. Skokie, Ill.: Rand McNally & Co., 1968. Grades 4-7.

CLARK, ANN NOLAN. *Along Sandy Trails.* Photographs by Alfred A. Cohn. New York: The Viking Press, Inc., 1969. Grades 2-5.

COLBY, CARROLL B. *Historical American Landmarks; From the Old North Church to the Santa Fe Trail.* New York: Coward-McCann, 1968. Grades 4-8.

COMOCK. *The Story of Comock the Eskimo, as Told to Robert Flaherty.* Edited by Ermund Carpenter. New York: Simon & Schuster, Inc., 1968. Grades 4-5.

COOKE, DAVID C. *The Planes the Allies Flew in World War II.* New York: Dodd, Mead & Co., Inc., 1969. Grades 5 and up.

CROWELL, ANN. *A Hogan for the Bluebird.* Illustrated by Harrison Begay. New York: Charles Scribner's Sons, 1969. Grades 3-7.

DALGLIESCH, ALICE. *America Begins: The Story of the Finding of the New World.* Illustrated by Lois Maloy. New York: Charles Scribners' Sons, 1958. Grades 4-7.

————. *Ride on the Wind.* Illustrated by Georges Schreiber. New York: Charles Scribner's Sons, 1965. Grades 1-4.

DAVIS, BURKE. *Yorktown, The Winning of American Independence.* Illustrated with photographs and maps. Evanston, Ill.: Harper and Row, 1969. Grades 5 and up.

DeLEEUW, ADELE. *The Girl Scout Story.* Illustrated by Robert Doremus. Champaign, Ill.: Garrard Publishing Co., 1965. Grades 2-5.

DICKINSON, ALICE. *The Boston Massacre, March 5, 1770: A Colonial Street Fight Erupts Into Violence.* New York: Franklin Watts, 1968. Grades 5-9.

ERDOES, RICHARD. *The Pueblo Indians.* With illustrations and photographs by author. New York: Funk and Wagnalls, 1969. Grades 5-8.

FALKNER, LEONARD. *John Adams: Reluctant Patriot of the Revolution.* Illustrated by Jerry Contreras. Englewood Clifs, N.J.: Prentice-Hall, Inc., 1969. Grades 5 and up.

FISHER, LEONARD EVERETT. *First Book Edition of the Declaration of Independence.* Illustrated by author. New York: Franklin Watts, 1960. Grades 3-4.

————. *The Papermarkers.* Illustrated by author. New York: Franklin Watts, 1965. Grades 5-7.

————. *The Schoolmasters.* Illustrated by author. New York: Franklin Watts, 1967. Grades 5-7.

————. *The Silversmiths.* Illustrated by author. New York: Franklin Watts, 1965. Grades 5-7.

————. *The Cabinetmakers.* Illustrated by author. New York: Franklin Watts, 1966. Grades 5-7.

———. *The Weavers*. Illustrated by author. New York: Franklin Watts, 1966. Grades 5-7.

FOSTER, GENEVIEVE. *George Washington's World*. Illustrated by author. New York: Charles Scribner's Sons, 1941. Grades 5-7.

———. *Year of Columbus*. Illustrated by author. New York: Charles Scribner's Sons, 1969. Grades 2-5.

———. *Year of the Pilgrim*. Illustrated by author. New York: Charles Scribner's Sons, 1969. Grades 2-6.

FREEMAN, MAE BLACKER. *Stars and Stripes: The Story of the American Flag*. Illustrated by Lorence Bjorklund. New York: Random House, Inc., 1964. Grades 2-5.

GEMMING, ELIZABETH. *Huckleberry Hill; Child Life in Old New England*. New York: Thomas Y. Crowell Co., 1968. Grades 4-9.

HARMER, MABEL. *The True Book of Pioneers*. Illustrated by Loran Wilford. Chicago: Children's Press, 1957. Grades 1-3.

HEUMAN, WILLIAM. *Buffalo Soldier*. New York: Dodd, Mead & Co., Inc., 1969. Grades 7 and up.

HOFSINDE, ROBERT (GRAY-WOLF). *The Indian Medicine Man*. Illustrated by author. New York: William Morrow and Co., 1966. Grades 4-7.

———. *Indian Sign Language*. Illustrated by author. New York: William Morrow and Co., 1956. Grades 4-6.

INGRAHAM, LEONARD W. *Slavery in the United States*. New York: Franklin Watts, 1968. Grades 6-9.

JOHNSTON, JOHANNA. *The Connecticut Colony*. New York: Crowell Collier & Macmillan Co. Grades 4-9.

KNIGHT, RALPH. *The Burr-Hamilton Duel, July 11, 1804; A Tragedy that Stunned the American Nation*. New York: Franklin Watts, 1968. Grades 5-8.

LEVENSON, DOROTHY. *The First Book of the Civil War*. New York: Franklin Watts, 1968. Grades 4-6.

McMAHAN, IAN. *Highlights of American History*. Racine, Wis.: Golden Press, Western Publishing Co., 1969. All grades.

McNEER, MAY. *Profile of American History*. Maplewood, N.J.: Hammond and Co., 1965. Grades 5 and up.

MIERS, EARL SCHENCK. *The Story of the American Negro*. Illustrated with photographs. New York: Grosset & Dunlap, Inc., 1965. Grades 6-8.

MONJO, F. N. *Indian Summer*. Illustrated by Anita Lobel. New York: Harper and Row Publishers, 1968. Grades 1-2.

NISENSON, SAMUEL, AND GOLLINGS, FRANKLIN. *Great Moments in American History*. New York: The Lion Press, 1968. All grades.

PETERSON, HAROLD L. *Forts in America*. Illustrated by Daniel D. Feaser. New York: Charles Scribner's Sons, 1964. Grades 5-9.

PINE, TILLIE S., AND LEVINE, JOSEPH. *The Indians Knew*. Illustrated by Ezra J. Keats. New York: McGraw-Hill Book Co., 1957. Grades 1-4.

———. *The Pilgrims Knew*. Illustrated by Ezra J. Keats. New York: McGraw-Hill Book Co., 1957. Grades 1-4.

POLITI, LEO. *The Mission Bell*. New York: Charles Scribner's Sons, 1953. Grades 1-5.

PUMPHREY, MARGARET. *Pilgrim Stories*. Edited by Elvajean Hall. Illustrated by Jon Nielsen. Skokie, Ill.: Rand McNally Co., Inc., 1962. Grades 4-6.

RICH, LOUISE D. *The First Book of the Early Settlers*. New York: Franklin Watts, 1960. Grades 3 and up.

SPEARE, ELIZABETH GEORGE. *Life in Colonial America*. Illustrated by Charles Walker. New York: Random House, Inc. Grades 5-9.

STEELE, WILLIAM O. *The Old Wilderness Road; An American Journey*. New York: Harcourt, Brace & World, Inc., 1968. Grades 6-9.

STERNE, EMMA (GELDERS). *The Long Black Schooner: the Voyage of the Amistad*. Illustrated by Paul Giovanopoulos. Chicago: Follett Publishing Co., 1968. Grades 5-8.

STRATTON, MADELINE R. *Negroes Who Helped Build America.* Boston: Ginn and Company, 1965. Grades 5-7.

TUNIS, EDWIN. *Colonial Craftsman: And the Beginnings of American Industry.* Illustrated by author. Cleveland: The World Publishing Co., 1965. Grades 6 and up.

———. *Indians.* Cleveland: the World Publishing Co., 1969. Grades 4 and up.

———. *Shaw's Fortune: The Picture Story of a Colonial Plantation.* Illustrated by author. Cleveland: The World Publishing Co., 1966. Grades 3-6.

———. *The Young United States.* Cleveland: The World Publishing Co., 1969. Grades 7 and up.

WELLMAN, PAUL I. *Indian Wars and Warriors; East: Indian Wars and Warriors; West.* Illustrated by Lorence Bjorklund. Boston: Houghton Mifflin Company, 1969. Grades 3-6.

———. *Race to the Golden Spike.* Illustrated by Lorence Bjorklund. Boston: Houghton Mifflin Co., 1961. Grades 5-7.

YOUNG, MARGARET B. *The First Book of American Negroes.* Illustrated with photographs. New York: Franklin Watts, 1966. Grades 4 and up.

OTHER LANDS, OTHER PEOPLE

BAHIJA, LOVEJOY. *Other Bible Lands.* Nashville: Abingdon Press, 1961. Grades 5-7.

BAKER, ELEANOR Z. *New Guinea: A Journey Into Yesterday.* Austin, Texas: Steck-Vaughn Co., 1968. Grades 5-8.

———. *The Australian Aborigines.* Austin, Texas: Steck-Vaughn, 1968. Grades 5-8.

BARCLAY, ISABEL. *O Canada!* Illustrated by Cecile Gagnon. Garden City, N.Y.: Doubleday & Co., Inc., 1964. Grades 3-5.

BERNHEIM, MARC AND EVELYN. *A Week in Aya's World: The Ivory Coast.* New York: Crowell Collier & Macmillan Co., 1969. Grades PreK-2.

BLEEKER, SONIA. *The Tuareg: Nomads and Warriors of the Sahara.* Illustrated by Kisa J. Sasaki. New York: William Morrow & Co., 1964. Grades 4-6.

BRENNER, BARBARA. *Faces.* Photographs by George Ancona. New York: E. P. Dutton & Co., 1970. Grades 1-3.

BUCKLEY, PETER. *Okolo of Nigeria.* Photographs by Peter Buckley. New York: Simon & Schuster, Inc., 1969. Grades 4 and up.

CALDWELL, JOHN C. *Our Neighbors in India.* New York: The John Day Company, 1960. Grades 2-3.

———. *Our Neighbors in Korea.* New York: The John Day Company, 1961. Grades 2-3.

CAREW, DOROTHY. *Portugal.* New York: The Macmillan Co., 1969. Grades 6-9.

CHUBB, THOMAS CALDECOTT. *The Venetians: Merchant Princess.* New York: The Viking Press, Inc., 1968. Grades 6-9.

COLE, WILLIAM, Editor. *Rough Men, Tough Men. Poems of Action and Adventure.* Illustrated by Enrico Arno. New York: The Viking Press, Inc., 1969. Grades 5 and up.

COMAY, JOAN, AND PEARLMAN MOSHE, *Israel.* Illustrated with photographs. New York: The Macmillan Co., 1964. Grades 5-9.

DOBRIN, ARNOLD. *Italy: Modern Renaissance.* Camden, N.J.: Thomas Nelson & Sons, 1968. Grades 6-9.

DOWNIE, MARY ALICE, AND ROBERTSON, BARBARA, Compilers. *The Wind Has Wings; Poems from Canada.* Illustrated by Elizabeth Cleaver. New York: Henry Z. Walck, 1968. Grades 4-7.

ERDOES, RICHARD. *Ireland: Bewitching Wonderland.* Illustrated with photographs by author and old prints. New York: Dodd, Mead & Co., Inc., 1968. Grades 5-8.

FORMAN, LEONA SHLUGER. *Bico; a Brazilian Raft Fisherman's Sons.* Photographs by Shepard Forman and the author. New York: Lothrop, Lee & Shepard Co., 1969. Grades 3-5.

GIDAL, SONIA AND TIM. *My Village in Spain.* New York: Pantheon Books, 1962. Grades 4-6.

———. *My Village in Switzerland.* New York: Pantheon Books, 1961. Grades 4-6.

HALSELL, GRACE. *Peru.* New York: The Macmillan Co., 1969. Grades 6-9.

HARRINGTON, LYN. *Greece and the Greeks.* Photographs by Richard Harrington. Revised edition. Camden, N.J.: Thomas Nelson & Sons, 1968. Grades 6-9.

HOWARD, CECIL. *Pizarro and the Conquest of Peru.* J. H. Parry, Consultant. New York: Harper and Row Publishers, 1969. Grades 6-9.

JOHNSON, DOROTHY M. *Greece: Wonderland of the Past and Present.* Illustrated with maps and photographs. New York: Dodd, Mead & Company, 1964. Grades 6-7.

KAULA, EDNA MASON. *The Land and People of Kenya.* Philadelphia: J. B. Lippincott Co., 1968. Grades 5-9.

KUBIE, NORA BENJAMIN. *Israel.* Revised edition. New York: Franklin Watts, 1968. Grades 5-8.

LINEAWEAVER, CHARLES. *Canada.* New York: Franklin Watts, 1968. Grades 4-6.

MCNEER, MAY. *The Canadian Story.* Illustrated by Lynd Ward. New York: Farrar, Straus & Giroux, 1953. Grades 5-7.

———. *The Mexican Story.* Illustrated by Lynd Ward. New York: Farrar, Straus & Giroux, 1953. Grades 5-7.

MAY, CHARLES PAUL. *Chile: Progress on Trial.* Camden, N.J.: Thomas Nelson & Sons, 1968. Grades 6-9.

MERRICK, HELEN HYNSON. *The First Book of Norway.* New York: Franklin Watts, 1969. Grades 4-7.

MILLER, RICHARD, AND KATOH, LYNN. *Japan.* New York: Franklin Watts, 1969. Grades 5-8.

PERKINS, CAROL AND MARLIN. *I Saw You From Afar: A Visit to the Bushmen of the Kalahari Desert.* Illustrated with photographs. New York: Atheneum Publishers, 1965. Grades 2-4.

POOLE, FREDERICK KING. *Southeast Asia.* New York: Franklin Watts, 1968. Grades 5-7.

REIT, SEYMOUR. *A Week in Hagar's World: Israel.* Photographs by Louis Goldman. New York: Crowell Collier & Macmillan Co., 1969. Grades PreK-2.

RITCHIE, PAUL. *Australia.* New York: The Macmillan Company, 1968. Grades 6-9.

RIWKIN-BRICK, ANNA. *Gennet Lives in Ethiopia.* Photographs by author. New York: The Macmillan Company, 1968. Grades 2-4.

ROBERTS, NANCY. *A Week in Robert's World: The South.* Photographs by Bruce Roberts. New York: Crowell Collier & Macmillan Company, 1969. Grades PreK-2.

ROSE, RONALD. *Ngari the Hunter.* New York: Harcourt, Brace & World, Inc., 1968. Grades 2-4.

RUTLAND, JONATHAN. *Looking at Denmark.* Philadelphia: J. B. Lippincott Co., 1968. Grades 3-6.

SCHLOAT, G. WARREN, JR. *Uttam, A Boy of India.* Illustrated with photographs. New York: Alfred A. Knopf, Inc., 1963. Grades 4-6.

———. *Naim, A Boy of Turkey.* Illustrated with photographs. New York: Alfred A. Knopf, Inc., 1963. Grades 4-6.

SINGER, ISAAC BASHEVIS. *A Day of Pleasure: Stories of a Boy Growing Up in Warsaw.* New York: Farrar, Straus & Giroux, 1969. Grades 7-10.

TOOZE, RUTH. *Our Rice Village in Cambodia.* Illustrated by Ezra Jack Keats. New York: The Viking Presss, Inc., 1963. Grades 1-2.

WEISS, HUGH. *A Week in Daniel's World: France.* Photographs by Sabine Weiss. New York: Crowell Collier & Macmillan Co., 1969. Grades PreK-2.

WHITE, ANNE TERRY. *Odysseus Comes Home From the Sea*. Illustrated by Arthur Shilstone. New York: Crowell Collier & Macmillan Co., 1968. Grades 5-8.

ZOLOTOW, CHARLOTTE. *A Week in Yani's World: Greece*. Photographs by Donald Getsug. New York: Crowell Collier & Macmillan Co., 1969. Grades PreK-2.

ART

FULLER, CATHERINE L., Compiler. *Beasts: An Alphabet of Fine Prints*. Boston: Little, Brown and Company, 1968. Grades 4-9.

MOORE, JANET GAYLORD. *The Many Ways of Seeing: An Introduction to the Pleasure of Arts*. Cleveland: The World Publishing Co., 1969. Grades 7 and up.

MUSIC

BULLA, CLYDE. *Stories of Gilbert and Sullivan Operas*. Illustrated by James and Ruth McCrea. New York: Crowell Collier & Macmillan Co., 1968. Grades 6-9.

DUNLOP, AGNES. *Duet: The Story of Clara and Robert Schumann*. New York: Holt, Rinehart & Winston, Inc., 1968. Grades 6 and up.

KAUFMAN, WILLIAM I. *UNICEF Book of Children's Songs*. Harrisburg, Pa.: Stackpole Books, Inc., 1970. All grades.

KRISVOY, JUEL. *New Games to Play*. Illustrated by Jerry Warshaw. Chicago: Follett Publishing Co., 1968. Grades PreK-1.

MITCHELL, DONALD, Compiler. *Every Child's Book of Nursery Songs*. Arranged by Cary Blyton. Illustrated by Ellen Howard. New York: Crown Publishers, Inc., 1969. Grades PreK-4.

UNTERMEYER, LOUIS. *Tales from the Ballet*. Illustrated by A. N. Provensen. Racine, Wis.: Golden Press, Western Publishing Co., 1968. Grades 4-6.

WECHSBERG, JOSEPH. *The Pantheon Story of Music for Young People*. New York: Pantheon Books, 1968. Grades 6 and up.

WILDER, LAURA INGALLS. *The Laura Ingalls Wilder Songbook*. Compiled and edited by Eugenia Garson. Illustrated by Garth Williams. New York: Harper & Row, Publishers, 1968. Grades 4 and up.

ABC AND COUNTING

BURNINGHAM, JOHN. *ABC*. Illustrated by the author. Indianapolis, Ind.: Bobbs-Merrill Co., 1967. Grades PreK-1.

CHWABT, SEYMOUR, AND MOSKOF, MARTIN STEPHEN. *Still Another Alphabet Book*. New York: McGraw-Hill Book Co., 1969. Grades PreK-1.

DUVOISIN, ROGER. *A for the Ark*. Illustrated by author. New York: Lothrop, Lee & Shepard Co., 1952. Grades K-2.

FALLS, C. B. *A B C Book*. Garden City, N.Y.: Doubleday & Co., Inc., 1957. Grades PreK-1.

GAG, WANDA. *The A B C Bunny*. Illustrated by author. New York: Coward-McCann, 1933. Grades PreK-1.

GRETZ, SUSANNA. *Teddy Bears 1 to 10*. Illustrated by author. Chicago: Follett Publishing Co., 1969. Grades PreK-1.

HAMANN, BENTE. *A Friendly ABC: French-English Alphabet*. Illustrated by Lorenz Froelich. New York: Frederick Warne and Co., 1970. Grades PreK-1.

IPCAR, DAHLOV. *Brown Cow Farm*. Garden City, N.Y.: Doubleday & Co., Inc., 1959. Grades PreK-K.

MILES, MISKA. *Apricot A B C*. Illustrated by Peter Parnall. Boston: Little, Brown and Company, 1969. Grades PreK-1.

MONTRESOR, BENI. *A for Angel: Beni Mintersor's A B C Picture-Stories*. New York: Alfred A. Knopf, Inc., 1969. Grades PreK-1.

MUNARI, BRUNO. *Bruno Munari's A B C.* Illustrated by author. Cleveland: World Publishing Co., 1960. Grades PreK-1.

PEPPE, RODNEY. *The Alphabet Book.* New York: Four Winds, Scholastic Book Services, 1968. Grades PreK-1.

REID, JON. *Celestino Piattti's Animal ABC.* Illustrated by Celestino Piatti. New York: Atheneum Publishers, 1966. Grades PreK-1.

TUDOR, TASHA. *A is for Annabelle.* Illustrated by author. New York: Henry Z. Walck, 1954. Grades PreK-1.

———. *1 Is One.* Illustrated by author. New York: Henry Z. Walck, 1956. Grades K-2.

WALKER, BARBARA K. *I Packed My Trunk.* Chicago: Follett Publishing Co., 1969. Grades PreK-1.

WILDSMITH, BRIAN. *Brian Wildsmith's ABC.* Illustrated by author. New York: Franklin Watts, 1963. Grades PreK-1.

EASY BOOKS AND PICTURE BOOKS

ANDRE, EVELYN M. *Things We Like to Do.* Nashville, Tenn.: Abingdon Press, 1968. Grades PreK-K.

ARDIZZONE, EDWARD. *Tim to the Lighthouse.* New York: Henry Z. Walck, 1968. Grades K-3.

BABBITT, NATALIE. *Phoebe's Revolt.* New York: Farrar, Straus & Giroux, 1968. Grades K-3.

BENCHLEY, NATHANIEL. *A Ghost Named Fred.* Illustrated by Ben Shecter. New York: Harper and Row Publishers, 1968. Grades PreK-2.

BROWN, MARCIA. *How, Hippo!* New York: Charles Scribner's Sons, 1969. Grades PreK-3.

BURCH, ROBERT. *Joey's Cat.* Illustrated by Don Freeman. New York: The Viking Press, 1969. Grades PreK-3.

CALHOUN, MAY. *The Goblin Under the Stairs.* Illustrated by Janet McCaffrey. New York: William Morrow & Co., 1968. Grades PreK-3.

CAUDILL, REBECCA, AND AYARS, JAMES STERLING. *Contrary Jenkins.* Illustrated by Glen Rounds. New York: Holt, Rinehart & Winston, Inc., 1969. Grades 1-3.

EMBERLEY, ED. *Green Says Go.* Boston: Little, Brown and Co., 1968. Grades K-3.

FISHER, AILEEN LUCIA. *Sing, Little Mouse.* Illustrated by Symeon Shimin. New York: Crowell Collier & Macmillan Co., 1969. Grades PreK-3.

FOSTER, JOANNA. *Pete's Puddle.* Illustrated by Beatrice Darwin. New York: Harcourt, Brace & World, Inc., 1969. Grades PreK-1.

FRITZ, JEAN. *George Washington's Breakfast.* Illustrated by Paul Galdone. New York: Coward-McCann, 1969. Grades 2-5.

GARELICK, MAY. *Look at the Moon.* Illustrated by Leonard Weisgard. New York: William R. Scott, 1969. Grades PreK-2.

GRIFALCONI, ANN. *The Toy Trumpet.* Illustrated by author. Indianapolis, Ind.: Bobbs-Merrill Co., 1968. Grades PreK-2.

GRIMM, JAKOB LUDWIG KARL, AND GRIMM, WILHELM KARL. *Little Red Ridinghood.* Illustrated by Bernadette. Cleveland: World Publishing Co., 1969. Grades PreK-3.

HOBAN, RUSSELL. *A Birthday for Frances.* Illustrated by Lillian Hoban. New York: Harper and Row Publishers, 1968. Grades PreK-2.

———. *Harvey's Hideout.* Illustrated by Lillian Hoban. Bergenfield, N.J.: Parents' Magazine Enterprises, Inc., 1969. Grades PreK-2.

HOLL, ADELAIDE. *The Remarkable Egg.* Illustrated by Roger Duvoisin. New York: Lothrop, Lee & Shepard Co., 1968. Grades PreK-2.

HUGHES, LANGSTON. *Black Misery.* Illustrated by Arouni. New York: Eriksson Publishing Co., 1969. All grades.

JOHNSON, ELIZABETH. *All in Free But Janey.* Illustrated by Trina Schart Hyman. Boston: Little, Brown & Co., 1968. Grades PreK-3.

JOHNSON, LAVERNE. *Night Noises.* Illustrated by Martha Alexander. Bergenfield, N.J.: Parents' Magazine Enterprises, Inc., 1968. Grades PreK-1.

KEATS, EZRA JACK. *Goggles!* New York: The Macmillan Co., 1969. Grades PreK-3.

———. *Peter's Chair.* New York: Harper and Row Publishers, 1967. Grades PreK-3.

———. *The Snowy Day.* New York: The Viking Press, 1962. Grades PreK-3.

———. *Whistle for Willie.* New York: The Viking Press, 1964. Grades PreK-3.

LEAR, EDWARD. *The Four Little Children Who Went Around the World.* Illustrated by Arnold Lobel. New York: The Macmillan Co., 1968. Grades K-4.

———. *The Owl and the Pussycat.* Illustrated by Barbara Cooney. Boston: Little, Brown & Co., 1969. Grades PreK-2.

LEXEAU, JOAN M. *The Rooftop Mystery.* Illustrated by Syd Hoff. New York: Harper & Row Publishers, 1968. Grades PreK-2.

LIONNI, LEO. *Alexander and the Wind-up Mouse.* New York: Pantheon Books, 1969. Grades K-3.

McGOWEN, TOM. *The Apple Strudel Soldier.* Illustrated by John E. Johnson. Chicago: Follett Publishing Co., 1968. Grades 1-3.

———. *Dragon Stew.* Illustrated by Trina Schart Hyman. Chicago: Follett Publishing Co., 1969. Grades PreK-3.

MAUGHAM, WILLIAM SOMERSET. *Princess September.* Illustrated by Jacqueline Ayer. New York: Harcourt, Brace & World, Inc., 1969. Grades 1-3.

MENDOZA, GEORGE. *The Gillygoofang.* Illustrated by Mercer Mayer. New York: The Dial Press, Inc., 1968. Grades PreK-1.

MILES, MISKA. *Nobody's Cat.* Illustrated by John Schoenherr. Boston: Little, Brown & Co., 1969. Grades 1-3.

MINARIK, ELSE HOLMELUND. *A Kiss for Little Bear.* Illustrated by Maurice Sendak. New York: Harper and Row Publishers, 1968. Grades PreK-2.

MUNARI, BRUNO. *The Circus in the Mist.* Cleveland: World Publishing Co., 1969. All grades.

PARISH, PEGGY. *A Beastly Circus.* New York: Simon & Schuster, Inc., 1969. Grades PreK-3.

PERRINE, MARY. *Salt Boy.* Illustrated by Leonard Weisgard. Boston: Houghton Mifflin Co., 1968. Grades K-3.

PIERS, HELEN. *The Mouse Book.* New York: Franklin Watts, 1968. Grades PreK-2.

PRESTON, EDNA MITCHELL. *Monkey in the Jungle.* Illustrated by Clement Hurd. New York: The Viking Press, Inc., 1968. Grades PreK-K.

RASKIN, ELLEN. *Ghost in a Four-Room Apartment.* New York: Atheneum Publishers, 1969. Grades K-3.

ROSENBAUM, EILEEN. *Ronnie.* Illustrated with photographs by Gloria Kitt Lindauer and Carmel Roth. Bergenfield, N.J.: Parents' Magazine Enterprises, Inc., 1969. All grades.

SHULEVITZ, URI. *Rain Rain Rivers.* New York: Farrar, Straus & Giroux, 1969. Grades PreK-2.

SPIER, PETER. *And So My Garden Grows.* Garden City, N.Y. Doubleday & Co., Inc., 1969. Grades 1-3.

———. *Hurrah, We're Outward Bound!* Garden City, N.Y.: Doubleday & Co., Inc., 1968. Grades 1-4.

STEIG, WILLIAM. *Sylvester and the Magic Pebble.* New York: Simon & Schuster, Inc., 1969. Grades K-3.

STOLZ, MARY (SLATTERY). *Say Something.* Illustrated by Edward Frascino. New York: Harper and Row Publishers, 1968. Grades K-2.

TITUS, EVA. *Anatole and the Thirty Thieves.* New York: McGraw-Hill Book Co., 1969. Grades PreK-3.

TURKLE, BRINTON. *Thy Friend, Obadiah.* New York: The Viking Press, 1969. Grades K-3.

UDRY, JANICE (MAY). *Glenda.* Illustrated by Marc Simont. New York: Harper & Row Publishers, 1969. Grades 1-5.

———. *What Mary Jo Wanted.* Illustrated by Eleanor Mill. Chicago: Albert Whitman and Co., 1968. Grades K-2.

VAVRA, ROBERT. *Pizorro.* New York: Harcourt, Brace & World, Inc., 1968. Grades PreK-3.

WABER, BERNARD. *Lovable Lyle.* Boston: Houghton Mifflin Co., 1969. Grades PreK-3.

WARBURG, SANDOL STODDARD. *Growing Time.* Illustrated by Leonard Weisgard. Boston: Houghton Mifflin Co., 1969. Grades K-3.

HISTORICAL FICTION

ALCOTT, LOUISA MAY. *Little Women.* Illustrated by Barbara Cooney. New York: Crowell Collier & Macmillan Co., 1955. Grades 5-11.

BRINK, CAROL RYRIE. *Caddie Woodlawn.* Illustrated by Kate Seredy. New York: The Macmillan Co., 1935. Grades 5-7.

BULLA, CLYDE ROBERT. *John Billington, Friend of Squanto.* Illustrated by Peter Burchard. New York: Crowell Collier & Macmillan Co., 1956. Grades 3-6.

CAUDILL, REBECCA. *Tree of Freedom.* Illustrated by Dorothy Morse. New York: The Viking Press, 1949. Grades 4-7.

CEDER, GEORGIANA DORCAS. *Little Thunder.* Illustrated by Robert L. Jefferson. Nashville: Abingdon Press, 1966. Grades 3-7.

CLEARY, BEVERLY. *Emily's Runaway Imagination.* Illustrated by Beth and Joe Krush. New York: William Morrow & Co., 1961. Grades 3-6.

COATSWORTH, ELIZABETH. *American Adventures 1620-1945.* Illustrated by Robert Frankenberg. New York: The Macmillan Co., 1968. Grades 4 and up.

———. *The Peddler's Cart.* Illustrated by Zhenya Gay. New York: The Macmillan Co., 1956. Grades 4-7.

DALGLIESH, ALICE. *Adam and the Golden Cock.* Illustrated by Leonard Weisgard. New York: Charles Scribner's Sons, 1959. Grades 3-6.

DEANGELI, MARGUERITE. *Thee, Hannah!* Illustrated by author. Garden City, N.Y.: Doubleday & Co., Inc., 1949. Grades 3 and up.

———. *Skippack School.* Garden City, N.Y.: Doubleday & Co., Inc., 1961. Grades 3 and up.

EDMONDS, WALTER. *The Matchlock Gun.* Illustrated by Paul Lantz. New York: Dodd, Mead & Co., Inc., 1941. Grades 5-7.

FALLS, THOMAS. *Canalboat to Freedom.* Illustrated by Joseph Cellini. New York: The Dial Press, Inc., 1966. Grades 5-9.

FIELD, RACHEL. *Calico Bush.* Illustrated by Allen Lewis. New York: The Macmillan Co., 1931. Grades 5-9.

FORBES, ESTHER. *Johnny Tremain.* Illustrated by Lynd Ward. Boston: Houghton Mifflin Co., 1943. Grades 7-11.

FRITZ, JEAN. *The Cabin Faced West.* Illustrated by Feodor Rojankovsky. New York: Coward-McCann, 1958. Grades 3-7.

GATES, DORIS. *Blue Willow.* Illustrated by Paul Lantz. New York: The Viking Press, 1940. Grades 5-7.

HUNT, IRENE. *Across Five Aprils.* Illustrated by Albert John Pucci. Chicago: Follett Publishing Co., 1964. Grades 5-9.

WILDER, LAURA INGALLS. *Little House in the Big Woods.* Illustrated by Garth Williams. New York: Harper and Row Publishers, 1932, 1953. Grades 4-7.

———. *Little House on the Prairie.* New York: Harper and Row Publishers, 1935; 1953. Grades 4-7.

MODERN FANCIFUL FICTION

ANDERSEN, HANS CHRISTIAN. *Andersen's Fairy Tales.* Illustrated by Lawrence Beall Smith. New York: The Macmillan Co., 1963. All grades.

————. *The Emperor's New Clothes.* Illustrated by Erik Blegvad. New York: Harcourt, Brace & World, Inc., 1959. Grades 2-5.

BARRIE, J. M. *Peter Pan.* Illustrated by Nora Unwin. New York: Charles Scribner's Sons, 1954. Grades 5-7.

BOND, MICHAEL. *Here Comes Thursday.* Illustrated by Daphne Rowles. New York: Lothrop, Lee & Shepard Co., 1966. Grades 3-7.

————. *Paddington at Work.* Illustrated by Peggy Fortnum. Boston: Houghton Mifflin Co., 1967. Grades 1-5.

BOSTON, LUCY. *A Stranger at Green Knowe.* Illustrated by Peter Boston. New York: Harcourt, Brace & World, Inc., 1961. Grades 4-6.

DE SAINT-EXUPERY, ANTOINE. *The Little Prince.* Translated by Katherine Woods. New York: Harcourt, Brace & World, Inc., 1943. Grades 3-7.

ENRIGHT, ELIZABETH. *Zeee.* Illustrated by Irene Haas. New York: Harcourt, Brace & World, Inc., 1965. Grades 1-4.

ERWIN, BETTY K. *Where's Aggie.* Illustrated by Paul Kennedy. Boston: Little, Brown and Co., 1967. Grades 3-7.

GODDEN, RUMER. *Little Plum.* Illustrated by Jean Primrose. New York: The Viking Press, 1963. Grades 3-5.

GOODWIN, MURRAY. *The Underground Hideaway.* Illustrated by Peter Parnall. New York: Harper and Row Publishers, 1968. Grades 2-6.

GRAHAME, KENNETH. *The Wind in the Willows.* Illustrated by Ernest H. Shepard. New York: Charles Scribner's Sons, 1954. Grades 5 and up.

HOUSE, CHARLES. *The Biggest Mouse in the World.* Illustrated by John Hamberger. New York: W. W. Norton & Co., 1968. Grades K-3.

KENDALL, CAROL. *The Gammage Cup.* Illustrated by Erik Blegvad. New York: Harcourt, Brace & World, Inc., 1959. Grades 3-7.

LAWSON, ROBERT. *Rabbit Hill.* Illustrated by the author. New York: The Viking Press, 1944. Grades PreK-1.

L'ENGLE, MADELEINE. *A Wrinkle in Time.* New York: Farrar, Straus & Giroux, 1962. Grades 5-9.

NORTON, MARY. *The Borrowers.* Illustrated by Beth and Joe Krush. New York: Harcourt, Brace & World, Inc., 1953. Grades 3-7.

————. *The Borrowers Afield.* New York: Harcourt, Brace & World, Inc., 1960. Grades 4-7.

PEARCE, A. PHILIPPA. *Tom's Midnight Garden.* Illustrated by Susan Einzig. Philadelphia: J. B. Lippincott Co., 1958. Grades 5-8.

RINKOFF, BARBARA. *Elbert, the Mind Reader.* Illustrated by Paul Galdone. New York: Lothrop, Lee & Shepard Co., 1967. Grades 3-7.

TRAVERS, PAMELA. *Mary Poppins.* Illustrated by Mary Shepard. New York: Harcourt, Brace & World, Inc., 1934. Grades 5-7.

WHITE, E. B. *Charlotte's Web.* Illustrated by Garth Williams. New York: Harper and Row Publishers, 1952. Grades 5-7.

MYSTERY

ADRAIN, MARY. *The Indian Horse Mystery.* Illustrated by Lloyd Coe. New York: Hastings House, 1966. Grades 3 and up.

ARTHUR, RORERT. *Mystery and More Mystery.* Illustrated by Saul Lambert. New York: Random House, Inc., 1966. Grades 5 and up.

BACON, PEGGY. *The Ghost of Opalina.* Illustrated by author. Boston: Little, Brown & Co., 1967. Grades 5-10.

BAUDOUY, MICHEL-AIME'. *Secret of the Hidden Painting*. Illustrated by Anne Carter. New York: Harcourt, Brace & World, Inc., 1962. Grades 5-7.

BAWDEN, NINA. *The White Horse Gang*. Illustrated by Kenneth Longtemps. Philadelphia: Lippincott & Co., 1966. Grades 4-6.

BONSALL, CROSBY. *The Case of the Hungry Stranger*. New York: Harper and Row Publishers, 1963. Grades K-7.

BORBHEGYL, SUZANNE DE. *The Secret of the Sacred Lake*. Illustrated by David K. Stone. New York: Holt, Rinehart & Winston, Inc., 1967. Grades 5-7.

BOWER, LOUISE, AND TIGUE, ETHEL. *Packy*. Illustrated by Herbert McClure. Nashville: Abingdon Press, 1967. Grades 3-7.

BRECHT, EDITH. *The Mystery at the Old Forge*. Illustrated by Charlotte Erickson. New York: The Viking Press, 1966. Grades 1-4.

BYERS, IRENE. *Mystery at Mapplins*. Illustrated by Victor Ambrus. New York: Charles Scribner's Sons, 1964. Grades 5-7.

CLARK, MARGARET GOFF. *Mystery of the Missing Stamps*. Illustrated by Vic Donahue. New York: Funk and Wagnalls, 1967. Grades 3-7.

ERWIN, BETTY K. *The Summer Sleigh Ride*. Illustrated by Paul E. Kennedy. Boston: Little, Brown & Co., 1966. Grades 3-7.

GOTTLIEB, ROBIN. *Mystery of the Jittery Dog-Walker*. Illustrated by Mimi Korach. New York: Funk & Wagnalls, 1966. Grades 2-6.

HITCHCOCK, ALFRED, Editor. *Spellbinders in Suspense*. Illustrated by Harold Isen. New York: Random House, 1967. Grades 3 and up.

HOLMAN, FELICE. *Elizabeth and the Marsh Mystery*. Illustrated by Erik Blegvad. New York: The Macmillan Company, 1966. Grades K-3.

JACKSON, JACQUELINE. *Missing Melinda*. Boston: Little, Brown & Co., 1967. Grades 3-7.

McGREGOR, R. J. *The Young Detectives*. Illustrated by William Grimmond. Baltimore: Penguin Books, Inc., 1934. Grades 3 and up.

PETERSON, JOHN. *The Secret Hide-out*. New York: Four Winds Press, Scholastic Book Services, 1965. Grades 3-5.

PLATT, KIN. *Big Max*. Illustrated by Robert Lopshire. New York: Harper and Row Publishers, 1965. Grades K-2.

SOBOL, DONALD J. *Encyclopedia Brown: Boy Detective*. Illustrated by Leonard Shortall. Camden, N.J.: Thomas Nelson & Sons, 1963. Grades 3-7.

ST. JOHN, WYLLY FOLK. *The Secrets of Hidden Creek*. Illustrated by Paul Galdone. New York: The Viking Press, 1966. Grades 2-6.

REALISTIC FICTION

ATWATER, RICHARD AND FLORENCE. *Mr. Popper's Penguins*. Illustrated by Robert Lawson. Boston: Little, Brown & Co., 1938. Grades 4-7.

BAUM, BETTY. *Patricia Crosses Town*. Illustrated by Nancy Grossman. New York: Alfred A. Knopf, Inc., 1965. Grades 4-7.

BERG, JEAN HORTON. *Miss Kirby's Room*. Illustrated by Alex Stein. Philadelphia: Westminster Press, 1966. Grades 4-7.

BONHAM, FRANK. *Durango Street*. New York: E. P. Dutton & Co., 1965. Grades 7 and up.

BURCHARDT, NELLIE. *Reggie's No-Good Bird*. Illustrated by Harold Berson. New York: Franklin Watts, Inc., 1967. Grades 3-7.

BUTTERWORTH, WILLIAM E. *Helicopter Pilot*. New York: W. W. Norton & Co., 1967. Grades 3-11.

CANTY, MARY. *The Green Gate*. Illustrated by Vera Bock. New York: David McKay Co., 1965. Grades 4-7.

CARLSON, NATALIE SAVAGE. *The Empty Schoolhouse*. Illustrated by John Kaufmann. New York: Harper & Row Publishers, 1965. Grades 2-6.

CRETAN, GLADYS YESSAYAN. *All Except Sammy.* Illustrated by Symeon Shimin. Boston: Little, Brown & Co. Grades 2-6.

DE ANGELI, ARTHUR AND MARGUERITE. *The Empty Barn.* Illustrated by Marguerite De Angeli. Philadelphia: Westminster Press, 1965. Grades PreK-2.

EMBRY, MARGARET. *Peg-Leg Willy.* Illustrated by Ann Grifalconi. New York: Holiday House, Inc., 1966. Grades 1-4.

ENRIGHT, ELIZABETH. *Gone-Away Lake.* Illustrated by Beth and Joe Krush. New York: Harcourt, Brace & World, Inc., 1957. Grades 5-7.

ESTES, ELEANOR. *The Alley.* Illustrated by Edward Ardizzone. New York: Harcourt, Brace & World, Inc., 1964. Grades 3-7.

———. *Hundred Dressess.* Illustrated by Louis Slobodkin. New York: Harcourt, Brace & World, Inc., 1944. Grades 5-7.

GEORGE, JEAN. *My Side of the Mountain.* Illustrated by author. New York: E. P. Dutton & Co., 1959. Grades 5-8.

HAYWOOD, CAROLYN. *Here Comes the Bus!* Illustrated by author. New York: William Morrow & Co., 1963. Grades 1-4.

HEILBRONER, JOAN. *The Happy Birthday Present.* Illustrated by Mary Chalmers. New York: Harper & Row Publishers, 1962. Grades PreK-2.

IPCAR, DAHLOV. *General Felice.* Illustrated by Kenneth Longtemps. New York: McGraw-Hill Book Co., 1967. Grades 3-7.

KRUMGOLD, JOSEPH. *And Now Miguel.* Illustrated by Jean Charlot. New York: Crowell Collier & Macmillan Co., 1953. Grades 5 and up.

LAFARGE, PHYLLIS. *The Gumdrop Necklace.* Illustrated by Alan E. Cober. New York: Alfred A. Knopf, Inc., 1967. Grades 2-5.

LENSKI, LOIS. *High-Rise Secret.* Philadelphia: J. B. Lippincott Co., 1966. Grades 1-5.

FITZHUGH, LOUISE. *Harriet the Spy.* Illustrated by author. New York: Harper & Row Publishers, 1964. Grades 5-9.

MCCARTHY, AGNES. *Room 10.* Philadelphia: Doubleday & Co., 1966. Grades 3-5.

MCCLOSKEY, ROBERT. *Homer Price.* Illustrated by author. New York: The Viking Press, 1943. Grades 5-9.

NEVILLE, EMILY. *It's Like This, Cat.* Illustrated by Emil Weiss. New York: Harper & Row Publishers, 1963. Grades 5-9.

PALMER, CANDIDA. *A Ride On High.* Illustrated by Rom Hall. Philadelphia: J. B. Lippincott Co., 1966.

ROBERTSON, KEITH. *Henry Reed's Journey.* Illustrated by Robert McCloskey. New York: The Viking Press, 1963. Grades 4-7.

SHIELDS, RITA. *Chris Muldoon.* Illustrated by Ray Abel. New York: David McKay Co., 1965. Grades 4-7.

SNYDER, ZILPHA KEATLEY. *The Egypt Game.* Illustrated by Alton Raible. New York: Atheneum Publishers, 1967. Grades 3-7.

STERLING, DOROTHY. *Mary Jane.* Illustrated by Ernest Critchlow. Garden City, N.Y.: Doubleday & Co., Inc., 1959. Grades 5-9.

WARREN, MARY PHRANER. *Walk in My Moccasins.* Illustrated by Vitor Mays. Philadelphia: Westminster Press, 1966. Grades 4-7.

SPORTS

ARMER, ALBERTA. *Screwball.* Illustrated by W. T. Mars. Cleveland: World Publishing Co., 1963. Grades 5-6.

BERGER, PHIL. *Heroes of Pro Basketball.* New York: Random House, 1968. Grades 6-9.

CHRISTOPHER, MATT. *Baseball Flyhawk.* Illustrated by Foster Cadell. Boston: Little, Brown & Co., 1963. Grades 4-5.

————. *The Year Mom Won the Pennant.* Illustrated by Foster Caddell. Boston: Little, Brown & Co., 1968. Grades 3-5.

COOMBS, CHARLES IRA. *Motorcycling.* New York: William Morrow & Co., 1968. Grades 4-6.

FENNER, PHYLLIS, Editor. *Crack of the Bat.* New York: Alfred A. Knopf, Inc., 1952. Grades 4-8.

FOX, LARRY. *Little Men in Sports.* New York: W. W. Norton & Co., 1968. Grades 6-9.

HOLLANDER, ZANDER. *Great Moments in Pro Football.* New York: Random House, 1969, Grades 5-9.

————. *Great Rookies of Pro Basketball.* New York: Random House, 1969. Grades 5-9.

LORD, BEMAN. *Mystery Guest at Left End.* Illustrated by Arnold Spilka. New York: Henry Z. Walck, 1964. Grades 3-4.

MONTGOMERY, RUTHERFORD. *Into the Groove.* New York: Dodd, Mead & Co., Inc., 1966. Grades 6-9.

OFFIT, SIDNEY. *Soupbone.* New York: St. Martin's Press, 1963. Grades 4-5.

RENICK, MARION. *Watch Those Red Wheels Roll.* Illustrated by Leonard Shortall. New York: Charles Scribner's Sons, 1965. Grades 2-4.

SEEWAGEN, GEORGE L., AND SULLIVAN, GEORGE EDWARD. *Tennis.* Chicago: Follett Publishing Co., 1968. Grades 5-9.

TOYE, CLIVE. *Soccer.* Illustrated by Paul Frame. New York: Franklin Watts, Inc., 1968. Grades 5-8.

UNITAS, JOHN, AND ROSENTHAL, HAROLD. *Playing Pro Football to Win.* Garden City, N.Y.: Doubleday & Co., Inc., 1968. Grades 5-9.

WHITEHEAD, ERIC. *Ice Hockey.* Illustrated by Paul Frame. New York: Franklin Watts, Inc., 1969. Grades 5-8.

YATES, BROCK W. *Racers and Drivers: The Fastest Men and Cars From Barney Oldfield to Craig Breedlove.* Indianapolis, Ind.: Bobbs-Merrill, 1968. Grades 4-6.

index